MW01640097

The Girl Who Couldn't Say No

Tracy Engelbrecht

For Ma, Mark, Conor and Layla. They know why

Prologue: I'll make it quick

This is the story of how I came to tell my parents I was pregnant at not-quite-fifteen years old. It's also the story of my life since then – how I turned out to be fabulously balanced, a single mother who really loves her life. I also do a mean lasagne. Did I mention the fabulous thing?

It's not a tragic cautionary tale of a Good Girl Gone Bad or even of Bad Girl Made Good… It's just a little story of changes and adjustment, of love and destiny. It's just my story. That should be good enough, I reckon.

Although I've always known I would write this (it's the creative equivalent of the Kellogg's All Bran Two-Week Challenge – with prunes), I could never find the words (nor the guts) to do so. It's just all so hard to express without sounding melodramatic and trite, or descending into girlish self-absorption. Heaven forbid the syrupy sort of Barbara Taylor Bradford "triumph against the odds" tale. It was never like that. I'd be lying if I told you it was.

There are lots of things I can tell you. I could tell you what you'd like to hear. I could tell you what you may expect me to say. Or I could tell the truth. The truth, of course, is harder, but it's the only way. Otherwise, what's the point? Even now, as I sit stuck on page one, where I have been for the past three months, I am suddenly terrified. Staring at this blank white screen, my palms are sweating and I'm suddenly sure, ***convinced,*** that I was wrong.

What the hell made me think that I have anything to say? Whatever gave me the idea that there's anyone out there who gives a stuff?

Deep breath. Sip of coffee. The moment passes. I remember that I don't hate myself anymore and that this is going to be fun. I think I'll be okay. We shall see. If you're reading this, then I did it.

I hope I get it right. For as much as this is my story, it's mine for only part of the way. After a while, it becomes my children's story too, and they will have to live it in their own way.

Maybe reading this will help all three of us understand what has brought me to where I am today, and what these past years have meant to me. And maybe this is also for anyone who has ever lived a life like mine, or will do so in the future.

Okay, so I'm also doing it for completely selfish reasons. As together and at peace as I tell myself I am, there are still some things that have never really been resolved in my heart, which I have yet to face properly. There's some scary stuff lurking around, and it's going to take a lot for me to get through it. If I don't chicken out, then it will undoubtedly be good for me, perhaps even saving me from years of expensive therapy.

But before we get to the juicy details, let me introduce you:

Who am I?

Ah, one of the ***big*** questions, subject of thousands of ***Cosmo*** articles and any number of dorky self-help books. It's a question that drives people to do strange and expensive things, like divorcing their spouses after thirty years to live in the Greek Isles with someone named Stavros. Or Candy. Or both. It's a question that some people pay other people vast sums of money to answer, while other people never even think of asking it.

I'm lucky. I ***do*** know. And I'm happy with the answer. Mostly. I mean, obviously, we're not talking about stretch marks and cellulite and certain obsessive-compulsive personality traits that could use some work. No, no. I'm talking about the me that has been me since the first time I was aware of being me. It took a long time, but I like her these days. You can make up your own mind, but you don't have to decide right away.

My name is Tracy (aka Mom-can-I? or Mommy-I-wanna!). I'm twenty-seven years old, and I'm a mommy. I'm a conscientious, if rather plodding worker. I'm not scared of snakes or bugs, but I'm very scared of driving. I'd give anyone else my last Rolo, but I'm still lumpier than I'd like to be. And I can write things that other people seem to enjoy. Not much, but it's a start. And it's all true, which has to count for something.

I'm no dynamic career woman. I don't network or do lunch – I work because I have to. My job does not define me, but I try to do it well. There are times I'd love to beat my boss (or myself) senseless with my stapler, but generally work is not unbearable and does not fill me with black dread when I get up in the mornings. It pays the bills (just), and gives me something to obsess over at 2am when I imagine I've made some horrendous mistake that will send the company crashing into bankruptcy.

I'm also no super-mom – I just do my best and hope that's good enough. So far, it seems to have worked. My children are allowed to watch TV and eat sweets and sleep in my bed. Sometimes, all at the same time. They drink Coke and make a noise but they are ***good*** people. They're growing up well – compassionate, insightful, smart and honest. And if getting there involves lots of ***Barney*** or ***Tomb Raider*** and sticky chocolate handprints on my sheets, that's okay.

What about my family?

There's my mother who is my best friend, my sounding board and my (occasional) metaphorical punching bag. We finish each other's sentences and argue over who has to make the next cup of tea.

My dad is the one who will say yes to anything, even things I haven't asked him yet. He doesn't say much, but I know how he feels. He plays golf. He just ***loves*** his golf. But being the kind of dad he is, he long ago stopped trying to explain it to me. He once told me that all men are dogs, and I should avoid brandy and Coke drinkers, because they're all hooligans. Very wise, my dad.

My sister, Emma, is my other best friend – she's beautiful, poised and braver than anyone else I know. She's pregnant with her first bean now and you'd think it was my baby, the amount of gratuitous shopping I've been doing. She's going to be a great mom.

Then there are my children, who are my reason for everything. Steven is nearly thirteen (my God, thirteen? Are you sure?). He's brilliant and gentle, could sell ice to Eskimos and can quote more Terry Pratchett at you than you'd think humanly possible. He's good at accents and uses words like "droll" in everyday conversation. He is the one who started it all. And he's special. He's on his way to great things and I hope the world is ready for him.

My special girl is Maria, five years old and a diva in training. She's strong and clever and independent. She's sweet and she's got ***attitude.*** By the bucketload. People melt at one look into those beautiful blue eyes, at that angelic face. She takes no shit from anyone and has already perfected the art of the dramatic exit (disgusted sigh, scowl, flounce, ***SLAM!).*** She's my Lallie, and I wish I could be more like her.

We have a dog named Ruby, who doesn't listen to anyone and who, I'm sure, needs some sort of doggy-Prozac. I try to remember how much she loves us when she's licking my bedroom carpet and eating my socks at 3am.

We also have two rabbits that run around the garden eating Froot Loops, grooming the dog and occasionally escaping onto the pavement. Watch in amazement as the whole family runs up and down the road in our pyjamas trying to herd wild-eyed fugitive bunnies back inside. This is done by means of long sticks and lots of shouting and lunging at fresh air. It must be fun to watch.

So that's us.

And they all lived together in a crooked little house. Well, not crooked, exactly. And it could use a lick of Ty Pennington (but then, who couldn't? That man is hot.). A different sort of family, but one that is happier and healthier than any other I know.

So, having said all that, dear reader, here we go. Ready?

Chapter One

1993: *In which she tries to explain herself and widdles on her shoe*

You'll have figured out by now that I had my son when I was fifteen years old. Yep, that's right. I was just a month shy of my fifteenth birthday when I found out I was pregnant. I was in grade nine and I had been – up until then, at least – A Good Girl. Quiet, reserved and painfully shy. No trouble at all to my teachers. Mostly invisible to my classmates. No real trouble to my family, although fourteen was a bad year for Mom and me. I'm sorry, Ma. I really am. I was difficult and obnoxious and sneered a lot. Much time was spent being what my mother called "awkward" and "otherwise".

I remember a look in her eyes when we fought, which I took to be anger and dislike of me. Now, as a mother myself, I realise it was a look of utter panic. Terror and dread of all that can go wrong – and you just ***know*** it will be your fault, because you're completely clueless. It was a look of "Fuckfuckfuck! She's not doing what she's supposed to. I'm messing up. What do I do now? Will someone please tell me what the hell I'm supposed to be doing?" Hanging on to your composure by a very frayed thread indeed, because everyone knows children can smell fear. If you let go for even one second, if your paper-thin veneer of Motherly Authority slips just an inch – they'll be on to you like a pack of hyenas. Gratuitous National Geographic feeding frenzy scenes will ensue. Especially daughters. Daughters are good at spotting the cracks and are handy with a crowbar.

I'm familiar with this look from the inside these days. I feel it in my own eyes sometimes, and I know it's only going to get worse. A sense of humour helps a lot. Once again, sorry, dear Ma. As penance, I promise to look after you in your old age. Bring on the bedpans – I deserve it.

There are people who think they have the whole "tragic teenage pregnancy" thing figured out. They don't. They don't know squat, in fact, unless they've been there themselves.

So, what can I tell you? That my childhood was traumatic? That it's all my parents' fault? That they didn't love me enough? Or loved me too much? That I was a wicked, wanton harlot throwing myself at anyone who'd have me? That I was an ignorant and naïve child, led astray by a bad older boy?

Sounds good, sounds like what you'd expect. Pick any of the above scenarios – we all have the makings of a juicy Virginia Andrews novel in there. Except, none of it's true. Sorry folks. It just wasn't like that. All the stupid things I did, all the typical teenage shit, were just a cunning disguise. Underneath it all I really was a Good Girl.

I always had glowing reports from my teachers; I did well without really trying very hard. I was definitely not one of the cool girls – but I wasn't totally nerdy either. Most of my classmates would probably have to think really hard if asked to describe me. I was just sort of nondescript. I was good at schoolwork, sucked at sports and wished that the Afrikaans ***mondeling*** had never been invented. In fact, if I never had to speak to anyone at all I'd have been happy. I spent most of my school years in a kind of permanent, whole-body cringe at my own ridiculousness.

I also had an overwhelming sense of ***waiting.*** I can clearly remember a time when I was about seven or eight years old. It was a beautiful sunny afternoon after school – that magical time around four o'clock: after homework, before supper – a time you were free to do anything at all, be anyone you wanted. I sat outside and listened to the birds. The air was still, there was no wind; it was quiet enough to hear the sea and the cars on the other side of the valley. There was a smell of "summer's coming" in the air. I still smell it sometimes these days, and I remember being seven. It was a special sort of day. The kind you remember for the rest of your life. You don't get many of those days. None of us do. Looking up at the sky, I remember feeling really small (maybe because I was?), and really sad. I remember asking, "Is this it? Is this all there is? Is there something else out there for me?"

Is there something else out there for me? No answer came. Not then. But I believed there had to be. Of course there was. Isn't there some unique, important destiny waiting for each one of us? I suppose I was impatient. I wanted it ***now*** – I prayed and wished and longed for "it", although I had no idea what "it" was. I spent years trying to find it.

I grew up with an anorexic self-esteem, minus the sparkling personality and self-confidence, if you'll pardon the generalisation.

Needless to say, I didn't have the slinky figure either. I thought that everyone else in the world belonged to some kind of fabulous secret society that I'd never be allowed to join. I felt as if I was on the edge of everything. Even when I was happy and having what passed for fun in those days of red jeans and Dr Alban, there was always some little part of me watching from the inside, reminding me that this wasn't real, this wasn't ***it.***

I looked for it in my friends, in books and in horrible, suicidal poetry. I looked for it where others seemed to have found it – the ones who seemed so cool and mature, the ones who seemed to ***know.*** I looked for it where they did – in cigarettes and alcohol, in boys and in obscure, depressing music.

Slowly it dawned on me that those kids who seemed to have it figured out – the ones who had found "it" – were just as lost as me. They didn't have it, after all. They were just as confused, just as unhappy and just as dense as I was. What they did have was lots of black clothes, proper Doc Martens and (some of them) expensive drug habits. I figured that out when I got myself the clothes, the boots and the Benson & Hedges, plus any number of over-exaggerated and embellished (in other words, untrue) tales of mysterious older boyfriends (plus a small assortment of real older boyfriends – handy, but not as mysterious), and still the meaning of it all eluded me. At the time, I thought maybe it was because I didn't have real Doc Martens. Maybe the Truth of the Meaning of Life, Ancient and Arcane Knowledge of the Great Unknowable Universe is handed down only to persons presenting with the correct brand-name footwear. If you turn up wearing Shoe City knock-offs, you don't get to pass Go and collect Infinite Enlightenment.

I began to suspect that there was nothing more to life, after all. That, yes, this ***was*** it, this dull and unimportant little life was all I could hope for. This, and more of the same – conversations about lipstick and boys and clothes – and variations thereof – forever and ever, amen. I was sad. Desperately sad. I was overcome by an enormous black cloud that I believed wouldn't go away, not ever. The one thing that I'd been holding out for my whole life – the prospect of something better, something more, something just for me – was gone.

I took an overdose of assorted pills one morning at school (God knows why I did it there – must have been the classic cry-for-help thing). I didn't think about dying, not really. I didn't think of how my family would feel. I wasn't thinking of anything much at all; I was too busy feeling. Feeling lost, raw, broken and sad. Having my head that far up my bum probably also made rational thought difficult. Somewhat muffled, you know?

I just wanted something to change. I wanted to turn the corner and come face-to-face with a parade – balloons and colour and a marching band with banners proclaiming, "Yes! You found it, Tracy! This is IT!" What can I say? I was fourteen. Fourteen-year-olds are dumb.

But I recovered quickly. Really quickly. Must have had something to do with the six kelp tablets I took – I mean, how was

I to know? No major damage done, except some to my relationship with my mother. She was deeply hurt by what I'd done and very, very angry with me. It took her a while to trust me again – and I think things were healed properly only after Steven was born. But I'm getting ahead of myself.

You probably want to know how I got pregnant. The usual way, as it turns out. What's to tell? Girl meets boy, much groping ensues and, well, you know how it all ends.

He was older than me and in college. He was a funny guy. He made me laugh. He lifted a little of the heaviness that had overtaken my life. My parents objected to the age difference, but I convinced them that it would be okay, that they could trust us. I thought so, too.

You know what it's like – you're on a diet, you think just a tiny bite of chocolate cake will be okay (after all, it's probably someone's birthday, somewhere in the world); of course you can stop after one little nibble. You tell yourself you're in control, you can stop anytime – and then, suddenly, everything goes black. When they find you, you're unconscious, face down, drooling into a cake tin with chocolate icing all over your cheeks and your jersey covered in sponge crumbs. The cake is history, of course.

What happened with David and me was something like that. It was awkward, consensual and over quite quickly – which is the best you can hope for at that age, I guess. It was also more or less inevitable. And before you ask, of course I knew better. Of course I knew about contraception – I was not ignorant or misinformed or pressurised. I knew it all.

Yet, at that moment, on the night in question, none of that seemed to matter very much. My usual sensible and responsible personality seemed to have taken herself off on holiday somewhere and the person she left in charge was a "whatever" kind of girl. I distinctly remember thinking this, that night in the dark: Whatever. It was so unlike me, a typical Virgo who usually analyses every situation, weighs up scenarios and consequences before eventually creeping along to a decision. I was a Good Girl, remember?

The Whatever Girl was a very temporary visitor. She buggered off shortly after, reappearing only once or twice since – when I least expected it, kind of like shingles. She didn't belong in my head and she knew it. She hung around just long enough to get me pregnant. But whether she knew it or not, she saved my life that night. I believe I would not be here today if it weren't for her. That black cloud would have swallowed me again and I don't think I would've found my way out. I would have given up the search for my one special thing. I would have missed my parade.

But she was there, she did what she was meant to do and, some weeks later, I walked out of the casualty section of False Bay Hospital. And there it was: my parade, with bells on.

I knew I was pregnant even before my period was late, in the way you do. When I was about a week or so late, I decided it was time to get real and find out for sure. I rounded up two of my best friends after school and off we went to the local hospital. The waiting room at Casualty was crowded – lots of sick, wounded, tired people. People far worse off than me, most of them through no fault of their own. Unlike me, the foolish clichéd statistic that I was.

I didn't know where to go, unsure how to go about this whole pregnancy-testing thing. I went up to a harassed and stern-looking nurse (they all looked harassed and stern).

"Excuse me," I whispered in my best Good Girl voice. No answer. She didn't even look at me. Perhaps she didn't hear me, I thought. I tried again. Cleared my throat this time, as it seemed to have become afflicted by a plague of frogs. "Excuse me, can you tell me where I should go for a pregnancy test?"

This time she did look at me and I know what she saw. She saw a kid in a school uniform (with a bright yellow name badge; we hadn't thought to take them off) playing at being grown-ups with her kiddy friends. She looked bored, irritated, pissed off. With me. Not used to being in trouble, I was a little taken aback. Then I realised that from now on, everybody was going to be looking at me that way – I'd damn well better get used to it.

"A ***what***?" she boomed, louder than I thought necessary. Nothing for it, I'd have to announce it to the entire waiting room.

"A pregnancy test, please." I was beginning to get pissed off myself, but Good Girls don't show it, oh no. Especially not when they deserve all the trouble they're in.

"See the sister down the passage, second door to the right," she snapped. She turned away, and I imagined that she couldn't stand to look at me any longer. A little melodramatic perhaps, but that's how I felt then.

Everyone turned to look at me – I felt the weight of their judgement on my back as I walked down the passage to the sister's office. Or imagined I did. Same thing, really, when you're fourteen and high on progesterone.

The same routine played out at the sister's office: "A ***what***? Really? ***Ag sies, man.*** Sister Du Preez! This girlie wants a pregnancy test. Give her the cup, would you?" And so on.

I was sure they were doing the whole scandalised, astonished thing on purpose. They must have seen hundreds of girls like me, many of them dodgier than me – but their job was to let me know what a fuck-up I was. What a failure. What a Bad Girl. As if I didn't know already.

Sister Du Preez handed me "the cup", a giant plastic funnel-shaped thing that looked like a tacky picnic wineglass circa 1983. I stared at it dumbstruck, thinking, "Where the hell does she want me to put this?"

"Shame, girlie", she said, not entirely nasty. "Don't worry, man. It's only to wee in. So we can test, you know? The bathroom is next door."

The blush started somewhere around my knees and crept on up towards my face. This was the first time I'd felt stupid as a mother, but it sure as heck wasn't the last. I felt tears prickling behind my eyelids, but I kept them in. There's that, at least. I didn't cry.

I made my way back past my friends towards the bathroom. I saw them eyeing "the cup" with trepidation and more than a little awe.

"Yes, look at me. Aren't I clever? I know what this is for. And I'm not a bit scared," I thought. I tried to convey all of this to them with a knowing and superior look as I passed.

Any sense of superiority I may have felt vanished as soon as I tried to wee in the cup. Only people who have done it would know how tricky this is. That glass was surely too tall for the job. I practically had to stand up to get it to fit under me. I obviously didn't line it up correctly because somehow hand, sleeve and floor got soaked. Yuck. Nevertheless, after a small yelp and a bit of jiggling I got it right and continued, stoic and resolved.

I was proud of myself, but my pride deflated a bit when I noticed my wet shoes and how little had actually landed in the cup. I spent the next few minutes trying to mop up the floor with six squares of government issue one-ply toilet paper (you just try it sometime). I may have been a disappointment to my family, a tragic example of wobbly morals and elastic virtue – but I'd be damned if I was going to leave a mess on the floor. I was still a Good Girl.

I carried the enormous plastic thing at arm's length in front of me, as you would the Holy Grail – or a giant cup of wee, for that matter. My future was in there, and I knew it. Quite a bit of my future was also squelching inside my damp school socks.

I handed the sample to the sister and she told me to sit and wait – she'd call me once they'd tested it.

"Don't worry, it'll be negative," twittered Amy, cheerily trying to be helpful. I gave her a look of utter disdain (probably unfairly), and she shut up pretty quick. I knew it would be positive. Of course it would be. My life was different from their's now. It simply was. The look I gave her was the first sign of the separation to come. I should have felt sorry, I suppose. She was only trying to be nice. I just felt annoyed with her, as the horrible nurse had been with me. Annoyed at a silly child who just doesn't get it.

We seemed to be sitting around for ages. People were coming and going, being called in to see doctors, getting bandaged up by the sister. New patients arrived and left again, hobbling, oozing, expectorating. And still we sat. Getting a little worried, I could wait no longer. I approached the nurse who'd sent me to the sister.

"Sorry, I know you're busy. I was here for a pregnancy test and they told me to sit and wait. Are they finished? Where should I go now?" Ever so polite, I was. I should have taped a "kick me" sign to my back right then.

The nurse looked me up and down, her eyes lingering on my name badge, which I now realised I should have taken off. I pictured her phoning the school principal during her tea break. I pictured myself being frogmarched off the school premises carrying a cardboard box of my stuff like fired employees do in the movies, running the gauntlet of jeering schoolmates and tut-tutting teachers, my humiliated parents waiting at the gate with a suitcase and a one-way ticket to a home for unmarried mothers in Klerksdorp…

This was what raced through my head in the time it took for her to look at my badge and say, "Oh yes, you. You're pregnant."

Just like that. In front of everyone in the waiting room, and as loudly as she possibly could without shouting. An she was loving every moment of it. Heads snapped around to check me out – this being a government hospital, there was no TV in the waiting room. They had to take their entertainment where they could find it.

Well, then. That's settled. I was calm, I think. Amy and Abigail were fussing and squeaking and doing those things that girls do. I didn't hear them. I also didn't hear Bitch Nurse From Hell when she told me to come back again the following week. Amy nudged me in the ribs and I woke up a little.

"Did you hear me, girlie?" grumbled Gestapo Nurse, now impatient. She'd had enough of me. "Sometimes it's a false positive. You should come back next week and do the test again to be sure."

I don't think I answered her. I was in a daze, more than a little gobsmacked. My friends steered me out of the hospital like an invalid or a drunk. I remember giggling. It's something I seem to do in times of extreme stress or shock. Giggle. No swooning, no violent tirades or even hysterical tears. Just daft giggles.

We walked back to the library, where my mother was due to fetch me. I'd told her I'd been doing research for a project on geomorphology. Ho-ho! There's a laugh. We didn't talk much on the way, we just giggled. Then Amy said, all concerned-like, "Don't go doing anything stupid now…"

I looked at her puzzled, not sure what she meant. Then I got it. Oh, she thought I was going to jump off a bridge, or OD on Dynajets. Given my history, I suppose I couldn't blame her. But suicide was the very last thing on my mind. My head was full of a million thoughts all twisted up together, pushing and shoving and fighting to be heard. ***How am I going to tell my parents-what about David-what about school-what about me-what do I do… What do I do…***

Among the confused jumble of panic, one thought was still. Lying curled up tightly underneath all the others was a tiny, quiet pink blossom of a thought, waiting for the fright to subside, waiting until I was ready to hear it.

I did hear it, once my friends had left and I sat waiting on the grass. I wasn't dazed anymore; everything seemed clearer, more real. The sky was brighter, the grass more prickly, the sounds around me sharper. More ***there***, somehow. Like I was seeing everything for the first time. I watched ants marching up a lamppost for a while, and they were fascinating.

Slowly my head started to empty a little, and that's when I heard it – just a whisper:

"This is it."

This was what I'd been waiting to hear all my life. It was real. I hadn't been crazy all these years. I'd known there was something else and now it seemed to have found me. Later, when everybody knew and there was so much unhappiness and recrimination, I began to doubt myself and nearly gave up. I almost believed that I'd been wrong. But just then, there on the grass, I knew. I remember feeling gratitude: faith that everything would be okay. And I remember strength in me that seemed to come from somewhere else.

"This is it."

***

As difficult as it was, I kept quiet while I waited for the second test. Because I'd been told to, I went back to the hospital, though I knew what they would say. I managed the wee cup much better this time, and in the months that followed, I became a pro. Not even a drop on the floor – I was ever so proud.

Bitch Nurse From Hell was not there this time, but Sister Du Preez was. She didn't seem so bad. When it was positive, as I'd known all along it would be, she told me to go and see the Family Planning Counsellor. Talk about shutting the barn door after the horse has bolted and is halfway to the glue factory! Nevertheless, you do as you're told.

"She can help you sort this out, lovey," Sister Du Preez told me before bustling off to berate a stabbing victim who was leaking all over the floor.

The counsellor was nice enough. As I sat down, she peered at my file, then looked back at me (school uniform again), and I didn't see judgement in her eyes. If it was there, she hid it well.

"So, you're pregnant? You're fourteen?" Nearly fifteen, I thought, but wasn't going to push the issue. Only children deal in half-years, after all.

"That's very young," she said, in case I hadn't noticed.

"Right," I said, all brisk and business-like. No time for messing about, let's get to the point. "And now what? What happens now, what are the procedures, where do I sign up?"

"For what, dear?" she asked, a bit surprised at my lack of denial and histrionics, which I think are the usual reactions. She glanced encouragingly at the box of tissues on her desk.

Nope, no tissues for me today, thank you very much. Today was all about getting things sorted out, settled, organised. Today was the day for making a plan.

"You know, sign up, for… um… whatever needs to be done…" I faltered. I thought I'd had it sussed: didn't you go to the doctor, get checked out for… um, things… and then, I don't know, learn breathing and stuff?

Apparently not.

The counsellor lady looked like she was trying hard to remember the extension number for the psychiatric ward. "The poor girl's obviously in shock", she must have thought. "She clearly doesn't know her arse from her elbow, probably a bit simple, in fact. Or it could be drugs…"

She spoke in the careful tones of one coaxing a stretchy-white-coat-wearing, bloody-scissors-wielding nutter away from the bodies. "Well dear, we've plenty of time for all that. You need to make some decisions first. Erm…" (Small hesitation here, choosing words carefully, not wanting to set off the looming nervous breakdown.) "…Do you know who the father is?"

Yikes. I knew she thought I was bad, but I didn't know she assumed I was such an abysmal loser. Visions of Appalachian hillbillies, dancing in her head.

"Of course I know who the father is, you bloody rude cow!" I wanted to screech, but didn't. What I did say was "It's my boyfriend, he's the only one it could be. It's just he's not here right now, because he… because…um, well…" My train of thought ground to a halt right there.

Because I'd told him not to come, that's why. Beats me why I did that. He knew where I was. He'd said he'd come if I wanted him to. We'd spoken about it and he was all about being supportive and doing whatever I wanted and "being there for me". He told me he'd "put me through school", though he was a little fuzzy on the details of exactly how he planned to manage that, or what it actually meant. He cried a lot. He was also all about waiting for the second test, in case the first was wrong. In other words, he was just hoping it wasn't true. He hadn't thought any further than that. He didn't know like I did.

I was all about being strong, being responsible, not needing him. And so I went alone. Still, he should have come with me, even though I told him not to. But at the time I thought it didn't matter.

The counsellor lady gave me an illustrated booklet about pregnancy and birth, and sent me on my way. She seemed relieved – I think I scared her a little. She told me to make an appointment at the antenatal clinic downstairs. I did so, self-consciously, although I didn't keep the appointment.

I went back to the library and sat at a table reading my precious booklet – hidden inside a large atlas, of course, in case anybody I knew happened by. There was a whole new world in there – one I'd never known existed. A world of trimesters and haemoglobin and scary-sounding things like pre-eclampsia and placental abruption. All explained in easy-to-understand, mildly condescending terms. I wanted to know it all. I tried to absorb as much as I could there in the library, because I knew it would be a while before I could bring my booklet out into the open.

I watched my mom as she drove up to fetch me shortly after. I smiled at her, and in my head I told her I loved her and I was sorry. I knew I had to tell her that night. I knew it would change everything, and there'd be no going back. For better or worse, my real life had begun.

***

Thirteen years later, it's still hard to think about that night. My friends thought I'd try to hide it. I mean, isn't that what you do? Aren't your parents supposed to kick you out, or send you to visit your "Auntie Cookie in Klerksdorp" (what is it with Klerksdorp?), or some variation on good old suburban ***skandaal*** theme? Someone even suggested I run away, rather than face my mom and dad. Apparently a life on the streets with a baby sounded terribly exciting. So made-for-TV-movie. Freaking Virginia Andrews again – she's got a lot to answer for, putting stupid ideas into stupid girls' heads. Although, call me Mary O'Flaherty and give me a job at the manor house, and it could even have made a passable Catherine Cookson.

But Sensible Tracy was back in control again. Not an ounce of romance in her soul, God bless her; she's practical and somewhat anal. She'd come back from holiday to find the place wrecked: cigarette burns on the carpet, vomit in the pot plants and strange people snoring on the couch. And she was not very fucking pleased, let me tell you. She bustled around angrily, picking up garbage and taking down names – and she decided there'd be no hiding the belly with giant jerseys or secretly giving birth in the bathroom. There'd be no more silliness. From now on, Tracy would be doing the right thing – you just watch me. From this day forward, for the rest of my life, I'd never give anyone the chance again to say I'd messed up.

Famous last words.

I called my mom to my bedroom after supper, saying I had to speak to her. I may have said I'd done something bad. Did she guess, or did I actually say the words? To be honest, I don't remember. But it was over quickly. She didn't shout or hit me or do anything dramatic. Maybe it would have been better if she had. The look on her face was terrible – shock, anger, fear and hurt. Lots of hurt. I imagined I saw hate there too – but I was too scared to ask. Some things you don't want to know. I certainly hated myself – to think I was the cause of that anguish on her face was almost more than I could bear. For years afterwards, every time the images crept into my mind, I'd have to physically shake my head to get rid of them.

Then she composed herself. I could see her take control, put her emotions aside and get a grip. I could see her mind working, making a plan, organising. I saw her remember that she was "in charge, damn it", and that she was the one who'd have to sort this out. I saw her stop feeling so that she could think. It was like looking at myself in a mirror. We're so alike – if it wasn't so godawfully horrendous it might have been funny. I wanted to hug her, to tell her how sorry I was, to tell her I wasn't bad, that I'd be good from now on, I promise. I wanted her to hold me and tell me it would be okay. I wanted to know that she still loved me.

But I couldn't ask her for those things. I knew I couldn't – I'd just have to let her say and do whatever she needed, and I had to take it. Hugs? For me? Not likely. Sorry, fresh out of hugs tonight, my girl.

I don't remember what we said, but I know I tried so very hard to keep calm – to show her how grown up I was, that I wouldn't resort to childish tantrums or tears. I remember biting holes on the inside of my cheeks and my fingernails digging into my palms until they bled. This is more difficult than you'd think. The marks on my hands were still there days later. Somehow I think my calmness made her even angrier. Maybe she thought I was proud of what I'd done – or worse, that I didn't get it. But I got it alright. Boy, did I ever.

"***You*** tell your father," she said as she slammed the door.

Oh God.

For some insane reason, I thought it might be easier to tell Dad. I thought that for all of five seconds – just long enough to tell him, "It seems you're going to be a grandfather sooner that you thought."

Crikey. Whatever possessed me to try and be all light-hearted? What an idiot. Early onset preggie porridge brain, maybe – or just wishful thinking. I mean, can you imagine trying to be funny about it? Jeez, for someone who's supposed to be intelligent, I can surely be thick at times.

Dad didn't stay calm – he freaked out completely. I think he shouted at me, and I've never been able to handle my dad being cross with me. As a child, I was proud of my ability to stare my mother down without crying, but one stern word from my dad and I'd crumble like a stale cupcake. And some stern words were spoken that night.

My big, strong father ran outside in tears. To see him like that broke my heart. I get nauseous just thinking about it.

Left alone in the lounge, I finally broke down. I cried that ugly cry – the loud one with all the drool and snot and heaving bosoms (such as they were). I cried until my face was swollen and my chest hurt. I cried until no more sound came out. My head felt like it had been bashed against a wall and my arms and legs were wobbly. The counsellor lady would have been relieved to see I wasn't freakishly self-controlled, after all. I now wished I had her tissues. My nose hurt from blowing it on scratchy toilet paper. Not government issue, but close enough for government work, as they say.

Then, just as quickly as the tears came, they stopped again. All cried out, I thought. Since then, I've learnt that there's no such thing. Just like there are always more socks in the washing machine than you think, so there are always more tears.

I couldn't sit still. Felt like I was going mad – I just wanted something to take my mind off it, something to distract me. I tried to read, but couldn't focus. The words just wriggled on the page and made no sense. I tried to watch TV, but my head was pounding and I was overwhelmed by waves of nausea. I wanted to be asleep, to hibernate unconscious until this was all over. If only I hadn't told them. If only I could go back to this afternoon, I could do it differently.

Sarcastic bully weighs in: "Oh yes? And just what did you have in mind? Exactly what would you have done? Run away? Kill yourself? Buy a really big jersey? Very mature. You really are a silly cow, aren't you?" Sensible Tracy was in the house, and she was having none of this crap.

“I don’t know what I would’ve done! But surely anything would be better than this! I feel awful! Everybody hates me! I’m really, really scared!” This was Sensible Tracy’s other half – her twin sister, Flaky Tracy. Flaky Tracy tends to wail and whine and daydream a lot. The two of them are always at it in my head, with occasional visits from lesser personae like the Whatever Girl.

Sensible and Flaky live together like a pair of lavender-scented cat-loving spinsters, arguing and sniping and eating Lemon Creams. Theirs is the constant battle between the romantic and the real, between wishing and planning, between “What Could Be” and “What Is”. Between espresso and decaf, chocolate and vanilla, Froot Loops and Weetbix.

“You know this was the only thing you could do. You’ve got to make this right. There’s no room for any further stuff ups, my girl. So what, if everyone hates you? You know you deserve it.” Sensible Tracy’s a good sort – she’s managed to keep me out of a lot of trouble, although I sometimes get the feeling she doesn’t like me very much.

Meanwhile, with all the drama going on, I’d forgotten about Emma, who was in her bedroom and must have heard the shouting. When I knocked on her door, she saw straight away that something was up. The puffy, red face and incoherent blubbering may have been a clue.

“What’s wrong? What’s going on?” Emma’s pretty little face was crinkled with worry. We used to fight, as sisters do, but we love each other. All of a sudden, I remembered how much.

“I’m pregnant,” I said quietly, as if whispering it would make it sound less incredible. She kind of gasped; her hand shot up to her mouth. And then she did something I’ve never forgotten – she hugged me. She held me tight and told me I would be okay. She made me feel safer than you’d think a small pixie girl of thirteen could do. In the midst of all that confusion and turmoil, even though I thought I didn’t deserve it, there was comfort for me. And I love her for that.

It definitely wasn’t easy for her, being the younger sister of “The One Who Got Pregnant”. Emma went into her teenage years with all that baggage; she carted it around with her for a long time, and that’s my fault. She got the fuzzy end of the lollipop more than a few times, but she didn’t complain. At least not to my face.

It was a long night. I answered their frantic questions about why and how and where and how could you, though not very well. What can you say? I had no real answers, no reason. No convenient tales of date rape or peer pressure. Not a millimetre of wriggle room in which to wail, “But it’s not my fault!” Because it was my fault, plain and simple. Any attempt to explain would just sound like an excuse. They didn’t feel my sense of predestination, of rightness and meant-to-be. They didn’t know there was a parade. If they did, they would have rained on it. If I’d waffled on about what a good thing this actually was, maybe throwing in a, “look on the bright side – at least I’m not dead, ho ho”, they’d only get angrier, because they’d think I wasn’t taking it seriously.

In the face of their disappointment and anger, I began to wonder if I had it wrong. My resolve began to slip, and that scared me more than anything else. The more they talked, the more I began to see what they saw: a life ruined, education abandoned, potential wasted. They saw all the problems; they saw all the "you can'ts". They didn't know about the list of "I musts" and "I wills" that I'd spent the past week compiling. And that night they wouldn't have believed me if I'd told them. As my parade slipped further away and the sound of the marching band faded into the distance, I panicked. Sensible Tracy floundered for a second and Flaky Tracy saw her chance. Unfortunately, this was just as my mother asked me, "And David? What does he have to say about this?"

Like the brainless twit that she is, Flaky blurted out, "He says he loves me!" All triumphant, as if that settled the matter.

Oy vey! Stupid bitch. As soon as I'd said the words I hated myself. Oh, how I wanted to bite off my treacherous tongue, to spit it out on the floor and jump on it, up and down, so that it would never be able say anything so ludicrous and embarrassing ever again. I would take a vow of silence and live on sour yak milk for the rest of my celibate life, if only I could take those pathetic words back. Only girls in soap operas say that sort of thing. It's irrelevant and silly and it's not as if I even believed it.

I was young and sometimes naive, but I did recognise my relationship with David for what it was: an adolescent fling that didn't mean much in the end, although we pretended it did. Isn't that what you do? Declare undying love and then forget each other after a couple of months? I knew that, but my soppy alter ego opened her big mouth to stick both feet in before anyone could stop her. That girl's face cries out for a good smacking. Now, what would Mom think of me? Oh God, just when I thought it couldn't get any worse.

Obviously she thought I was an irresponsible tramp with no self-respect: I could just about live with that. But to have her think I was a hopeless romantic fool as well? That was just too much. Too late. The words were out and Flaky sat back feeling smugly pleased with herself. Not for long, though, because Sensible stepped in and hit her on the back of the head with a frying pan and she fell down unconscious. That's Sensible Tracy for you – always prepared to do the jobs that need doing – the hard ones, the ones no one else wants to do. I suspect she enjoys them more than she lets on. Flaky was out of it for weeks, and what a good thing, too. I never would have got anything done with her hanging about blubbering and squeaking all over the place. For one thing, she wrings her hands and bleats way too much. It's just annoying.

I don't think anybody slept very much that night – except me. I was out as soon as my head hit the pillow. Exhausted and somehow hollow, I think my body took over and shut down all non-essential functions, such as thinking and possibly breathing.

You know the saying, "It'll all look better in the morning"? Well, it didn't. But it ***was*** the first day of the rest of my life.

Chapter Two

1993: In which she escapes ritual sacrifice, but not the speculum

I woke up with a stuffy head and a soaked pillow. For a few, blank seconds I thought I'd developed flu overnight. I felt hung over, my whole body stiff from lying in the same position all night. And what's with the curious marks on my hands? Fragments of memory floated around my head. Like a dream that evaporates as soon as you open your eyes. Hmmm… something's fishy around here. Fishy and slippery as a bugger. I just… couldn't… catch it… It took a few more seconds for the fuzziness to clear, and then I remembered. Oh shite!

There was no question of going to school that day; I was too wiped out. Felt like a zombie. I think we all did. Plus I looked like a freak with my still swollen, bloodshot eyes and matching sets of luggage plastered to my face. Bags under the eyes doesn't even begin to describe it. It was diabolical – I never knew a person could look that bad and not be oozing into a body bag somewhere.

But worse, the God of Teenage Mothers had decided that today was a great day to unleash the hellish monster that is morning sickness. I spent most of the morning hanging over the toilet, dry heaving until it felt as if my innards would explode out my ears (and the afternoon too – where the moniker, "morning sickness", comes from I do not know.). Every moment not spent gazing forlornly into the toilet bowl was spent sitting over it, because that minor pregnancy niggle of needing to wee every ninety seconds had also reared its nasty little head. I'd like to chat to the sadistic bitches who call it minor, by the way. It felt pretty major to me when racing to the loo for the sixteenth time in half an hour with a seemingly bursting bladder – only to find that said bladder contained exactly one trickle and three drops. Again.

What, with all the crying and weeing that followed over the next few weeks, a severe toilet paper shortage developed in our house. I notice the pregnancy books never mention the feeling of bleakness that overcomes you as you tear the last square off the roll at three in the morning. Twinsaver Rage, I think it's called.

I don't know why all these textbook symptoms hadn't started earlier. Maybe my body was waiting until all was out in the open, so that I could vomit freely without arousing suspicions of bulimia or cholera. Very considerate, you might think if you wanted to be philosophical about it. Although it's hard to be philosophical with your head in the toilet. I bet Socrates never had that problem, but then again, he never had a toilet, nor a uterus.

No school, then, thank God. Instead, my mother and I went off to the doctor for a confirmation test (all together now: "Maybe they made a mistake…"), and then the plan was to sit down to a conversation about My Options. I don't know how she got organised so quickly. My father was a military man, which meant we were all treated by military doctors. Handy, as it's free, but best you never suffer from anything that a Cepacol throat lozenge won't fix. Tonsillitis? Athlete's foot? Leprosy? Have a Cepacol. Cutting edge it was not, and it is also notoriously difficult to get an appointment with those camo-wearing doctors Same day service, in particular, was unheard of. Unless you arrived with an arm or leg in a plastic bag, you had to wait at least two weeks to get an appointment. Even then, there had better be lots of ice in that plastic bag, because you'd be waiting a long time. And don't bother trying to phone. If by some lucky accident the number actually worked, they probably wouldn't answer, because it would be teatime. Or lunchtime. Or everybody would be on a management course, or the place would be closed for fumigation. If it's free, the service is allowed to be crap. Well-known fact.

But somehow Mom managed to get me to the doctor that very day. Traditionally, in our family, she deals with those delicate Telkom complaints or rat-in-the-KFC type situations that require a firm hand, especially after others have tried in vain. This routine is known in our house as sending in the heavies. I've never got the hang of it myself.

I would have thought there'd still be much wailing and gnashing of teeth, but no. That's my mom for you. She's never been one for wailing. Thinking back, maybe she should have permitted herself at least some minor clothes renting and chest beating. She was due some freak-out time, but she never took it. She was too busy being Sensible. Maybe it would have been easier on her if she had let go a little then. Nobody would have blamed her. It's obvious that I inherited Sensible Tracy from her (why, then, not her skinny figure or supersonic metabolism, as well?).

We waited for the doctor in silence. Silence would become a pattern those early days. There was too much to be said and we didn't know how. It was a bad time for small talk. When my name was called, we made our sheepish way to the sister's office. I felt like I had a flashing neon sign above my head: "Watch Out – Pregnant Girlie Coming Through!" Maybe they should have just given me one of those lepers' bells. Picture me shuffling along in a brown Friar Tuck habit: "Unclean! Unclean!" Ding dong.

My mom quietly reported the reason for our visit to the nurse, who made her repeat herself louder, as per standard nursing practice, at least twice. She then went off to speak to the doctor and I was handed another huge, plastic wee glass. Old hand that I was, I took it and stalked off to the loo as if I'd been doing it all my life. No matter how old they are, eventually all pregnant women develop an air of resigned dignity – nothing can ever embarrass them again. Dinner party conversation turns ugly if you have more than one pregnant or recently pregnant woman present. Floaty bits in urine sample? That's nothing. Sixteen episiotomy stitches through three layers of tissue? Piece of cake. Emergency enema? Pish. Bring it on. We are superwomen. We love this stuff. Compared with the other paranoid horrors of first-time pregnancy, weeing into a wineglass seems delightfully tame.

I managed the manoeuvres fine this time, but it took ages because of the "one-trickle-and-three-drops" deal. I stood by and watched as a very young looking nurse tested the sample. I think she was about to start a rousing jazz version of, "maybe it's negative" – but she saw my face and changed her mind. True as cookies, the little pink lines showed up immediately, pinker than ever. You could call it cerise, even.

"Yes, it's positive. You're definitely pregnant," Young Nurse reported helpfully. Um, yes. I know. Thanks.

A whole bunch of standard antenatal tests followed. There was the usual pricking of the finger to test haemoglobin levels, with a malfunctioning needle gun thing. She had to shoot me three times before she got it right. I was about to go and find her a stapler to use instead, but then, hallelujah! The tiny smear of blood on the glass told her I was so anaemic as to be nearly dead. This was bad, I knew. I'd been reading my booklet, you see. I got all tearful suddenly. "How bad is that? What does it mean? Is everything okay?" I croaked.

"Don't worry, bokkie. We'll give you some iron pills and you'll be fine. And baby too." She smiled and squeezed my shoulder. It was the first time anyone had mentioned "the baby". So far, it was just called "The Situation". Nobody had gotten as far as thinking about the actual baby. I was so grateful for that that I almost started bawling again. Along with the morning sickness and bladder control, indiscriminate howling was another new development that day. Later, I cried when I couldn't find any mayo in the fridge, and then I cried when I did find it. I cried watching starving orphans on the news and buxom blondes on ***Baywatch.*** Apparently, this is normal and all down to hormones. I thought I was going nuts.

Then it was time to be weighed, which wasn't that bad, and have my first ever internal examination, which was extremely bad. The gynaecologist was a scary old woman with sharp, bony fingers and an Eastern European accent. She would not have been out of place in a gingerbread house. She poked and prodded with her freezing hands and creepy silver implements, then left me to languish with my legs around my neck and my nethers flapping in the breeze, while she went off to have a cup of tea or boil a small child in oil or something.

She came back eventually and seemed surprised to find me still lying there, half naked.

"Vell, get dressed. Ve are finish now," she cackled. Okay, so maybe it was a chuckle. It seems she hadn't gone off for a spot of human sacrifice, after all. She had just left the room so that I could get dressed again. Duh! I would have slapped my forehead if my hands weren't busy covering various outlying regions. It didn't make sense, really, as she'd just seen all the bits worth seeing. What difference did it make if she saw them again in the process of being covered up? But there you go. That's how things are done. You live and learn, and if you can provide perfect strangers with a little entertainment along the way, so much the better.

She looked like a seventy-five-year-old Elizabeth Bathory, had the latter not been walled up inside her castle and left to starve to death. Anyway, as I clearly wasn't a virgin, she wouldn't have been interested in bathing in my blood. This should have made me feel better, but no. She gazed at me over the tops of her gnarled, steepled fingers. She was scary. Then she got scarier.

"Now ve do ze blud," she intoned in her creaky Transylvanian voice. Excuse me? Ze blud? What the hell?

Trying to restrain my ridiculous imagination, I managed to stutter, "Um, but the nurse already checked my blood. She pricked my finger…"

She cackled again. No really, this time I swear it was a cackle. "Zilly chile, zat vas only ze aitch-bee. Now ve test for all ze ozzer tings." Small pause, while I translated sinister witch talk into English.

"Oh, the HB. I see. So now we do more tests?" I smiled in what I hoped was a non-threatening and, above all, non-virginal way.

"Yes. Nurze vill take more ze blud, and zen ve talk, okay?"

Okay. Then we talk. Woo-hoo!

I went off with Young Nurse to "take more ze blud". She ushered me into what looked and smelled like an operating theatre – I checked for iron maidens and suspicious looking vats but didn't spot any. My eyes watered from the overwhelming smell of pink industrial-strength disinfectant and the faint whiff of the reason for the disinfectant. Bleeergh…

I sat on a rickety metal stool next to a rickety metal bed and stuck out my arm as instructed. Then she started whacking me on the inside of my elbow and muttering to herself. I was a bit taken aback by this – it really stung. Bear in mind I wasn't used to these technical medical procedures. Still, when in Rome and all that.

"I can't find a bloody vein. We'll have to try the other arm. Give here," she said.

What? No vein? Surely you need veins? Where are mine, then? This was a worrying development. She tied a bondage-like blood pressure cuff around my other arm, and tightened it until it was a satisfactory shade of purple and I couldn't feel my fingers. Then she started smacking me again. I couldn't feel it this time, as all the nerve endings in my arm had withered and died.

"Ah! Here we go. Found one." She didn't warn me before sticking the needle in, so I didn't look away. Some people have no problem with needles entering their bodies. Apparently I do. A big one. Little twinkly lights flashed in front of my eyes and my stomach lurched. The ghost of breakfast past (one mealy Golden Delicious apple) was getting restless. I was still watching as she grunted in irritation and jiggled the needle around like she was stirring stodgy fruitcake batter. Urg…

The last thing I heard before I hit the floor was, "No bloody veins, man! Pass that other arm again…"

When I came to, I was lying flat on my back with a bright spotlight shining directly into my eyes. I couldn't see anything and for a second I couldn't feel my legs either. Then I felt something tube-like being pulled from my hand – it was hot and cold at the same time and very sore. I nearly panicked. Okay, I totally panicked. I think I may have screamed. Somehow, I'd managed to convince myself that I was in a sort of government-interrogation-slash-torture facility somewhere in Central America. Then I heard a voice. It took a moment to realise that it didn't belong to a greasy, cigar-chomping general named Salvador. And it wasn't saying anything like, "Dee bluepreents! Where ees dee bluepreents? Talk now and we won't keel youse… Enrique! Fetch dee clamps! Hur hur hur…"

It was my young nurse. "Hey, Tracy. You're okay. You just fainted, sweetie. We've taken the blood from the artery in your wrist instead. It's all over."

More crying from me. I was so relieved to find that I hadn't in fact been sacrificed in a satanic ritual, nor had any sort of encounter with a red-hot poker. Her squeaky voice was comforting – just like your mother's when you're five years old. I looked at her baby face and saw she wasn't that much older than me. She must have been a student nurse. And she was so kind. Boo-hoo-hoo! Again.

I sat up and sipped the water she gave me. Then I realised what an absolute tosser I'd made of myself. I groaned. Oh, my God! Who makes such a fuss over a little needle? I was so embarrassed, I would gladly have hopped onto that sacrificial altar if it meant I didn't have to see any of those people ever again. Boo-hoo-hoo! Yet again.

"I'm s-s-sorry… I'm really s-s-stupid!" I wailed. Hormones and nausea and self-loathing boogied together in psychedelic Technicolor and turned me into a quivering, drooling, snot-oozing wreck. I knew this wasn't making me look any less psychotic, but I couldn't stop crying. Until I had to – to vomit into a handy metal dish. I hung over that dish for some time, long enough to realise it was the type they used during operations to catch gallstones or appendixes or other diseased, squishy bits… Imagining the previous tenants of the metal dish, my stomach did a Highland Fling, then double, half-pike somersault. Lock of hair fell out of ponytail and into vomit. Realised I had vomit in my hair. Appalled. Vomited again.

And so it went. They eventually managed to suck nine test tubes of blood out of me that day. ***Nine!*** Can you believe it? They tested my blood type, Rh factor (One of those things I'd heard of but didn't know what it actually was, as such. Like emo, or tantric sex), HIV and syphilis. They told me they tested all pregnant women for syphilis. That had better be true, otherwise I'm seriously insulted. But that accounts for only four test tubes. What about the other five? I'm sure they needed them all for official, health-related purposes. I'm almost positive they didn't drink any of it from an oversized silver chalice, and they certainly didn't bathe in it. You'd need at least a hundred test tubes to get any sort of depth in the tub.

At last, the blood-taking ordeal was over. I had more blood drawn throughout my pregnancy, and it was horrible, but never as bad as the first time. But my veins were always (and are still) totally invisible to the naked eye and only accessible by means of a magnifying glass and a chisel. I don't hate the procedure as much as I used to, but would still probably choose the red-hot poker, given the choice.

Young Nurse went off on a tea break (teatime is the central theme in the civil service, as I think I mentioned before), so an older nurse took me back to Dr Evil's office. She was short and dumpy with a face like a happy raisin. No-nonsense grey hair, military haircut and military-issue glasses. A definite beefiness about the arms, implying years of manhandling difficult patients. Even snivelling hurlers like me. This lady could make you take your medicine. And you'd ***like*** it. She was the personification of bossiness. She was tiny and domineering and loud. And yet, everybody we passed seemed to know her and love her. She greeted everyone and stopped to chat with a couple of patients in the hallway. She knew everything about everybody and actually seemed to care.

Of course she intimidated me, so I kept my mouth shut and walked. She seemed about to say something. I held my breath.

"So…" she paused. Right, here it comes. The $64,000 question. I braced myself to be annoyed.

"So… I really don't see what the big deal is," she remarked casually. "I mean, you're old enough, don't you think? Everyone should stop freaking out."

Erm … excuse me? What was that? I couldn't believe my ears. I'd always wanted the chance to use the word incredulous in a sentence (even in my own head) – and here it was. Had to stop walking, in case I tripped over my chin as it hit the floor. Was she mad? Was she being sarcastic? Even worse, was she trying to Put Me At Ease?

As excruciating as it was, she probably ***was*** trying to make me feel better. And it worked, after a while. She stayed with me (having no young sailors to bully just then) and chatted idly about all the young mothers she'd known. No one tragic, just ordinary girls like me.

"So, you're keeping the baby?" she asked. I nodded.

"Yes I am." To be honest this was news to me. She'd caught me off guard and got me to say what I really wanted without trying to figure out how it would sound. Even so, I said it quietly, waiting for the torrent of "yes, buts…" that would come. There weren't any. She just nodded: ***of course*** I was keeping the baby. As if it was a silly question really.

"That's good. You'll be fine, you'll see."

Later, I sat back on the sticky leather chair opposite the doctor. As threatened, she spoke at length about "My Options". There was a firm emphasis on what a good idea adoption was, as it would just not be possible for me to be a mother at my age. I just Wasn't Ready, she informed me gloomily. I listened, but I'd been through all of this already on my own. For days now, this was all I'd been thinking about. I'd already considered all the usual options, swinging wildly from one harebrained scheme to the next.

I listened to her predicting my future: a wasted life of resentment and waitressing, head lice, ringworm and Child Welfare visits… And I thought I was a drama queen? I noticed a certain juvenile defiance creep into my attitude and posture. Arms folded across my chest, eyes downcast, lip curled, proving the doctor right with every sulky roll of my eyes. And pissing her off, too. I was exactly as immature and stupid as she'd thought. Fortunately, Sensible Tracy spotted this turn in demeanour and wasn't about to let me stuff things up. She kicked me hard on the ankle and I sat up straight, Moody Teenage Tracy banished back to her playpen. For now, at least. Moody Teenage Tracy was to grow up eventually: she became Moody Grown-Up Tracy, the only difference being that she now knows bigger words and nobody can send her to her room. I'm looking forward to Moody Middle-Aged Tracy and Moody Mouldering Ruin Tracy one day, too. It all sounds like a ton of fun.

No matter what this miserable doctor or anybody else had to say, I'd already decided. The decision had been made the night the Whatever Girl hijacked my body and my brain. Maybe even long before that.

However, a decision is not a plan. Any self-respecting Virgo can tell you that. I'd hoped to go to my parents with a good, solid five-year projection. With bar graphs. Spiral-bound, maybe. Unfortunately, a five-minute plan was as far as I'd got. It started with a trip to the loo.

I'd wanted to be ready when they asked the Big Questions. (Not "Who am I?" That one had already been answered, in my own mind, at least. I was "Tracy The Slutty Pregnant Slag, A Burden On Her Family And Society At Large".) But there were more pressing matters to attend to, such as, "What the hell did you think you were doing?" And "I hope you're proud of yourself now." What can you say to questions like that? Nothing very satisfactory, I'm afraid. They're not real questions anyway. They're just something to say to kill time while your head catches up with events.

The $64 000 question, the number one question I was asked by everybody back then (including friends, nuns and random strangers) and am still asked to this day is, "Where's The Father?" I have some theories about why people do this. I think it's the same reason people watch Jerry Springer. They do it so that they can pretend to feel shocked at what the world is coming to. They ***want*** me to look uncomfortable and admit I don't know who he is. Or just look at my feet and start crying. They want me to be a Bad Girl. And if I'm not a Bad Girl, then I must be a Stupid Girl. Either will do. Either would prove that they're better than me. They know they are, of course, but they want to hear me say it.

It's stupid, but it still bothers me, even today. Never mind my mothering skills, never mind what kind of life I'm giving my child, never mind how good we are for each other. I could be crowned Mother of the Year. I could give my child one of my kidneys or rescue him from a burning building. It would never be enough for them, just because I don't have that blasted ring on my finger. And even if I did get married one day (the day monkeys fly out of my butt – watch this space), those damn busybodies will still tsk-tsk knowingly among themselves, because that would just be a consolation prize, wouldn't it? I'm not fooling anyone, am I? It's second best and it's so unfortunate. (I hate that word – "unfortunate". It's like nails on a blackboard to me. I can't stand people who use it to describe other people's lives. They make me think unkind thoughts.)

Some people are just nosy and I try not to be bothered by them. It's difficult, but I'm making progress. When the bad thoughts come, I just smile, breathe and avoid blunt instruments. There are some people walking the streets today who don't know how close they've come to Death by Enraged Unfortunate Teenage Mother. Smile and breathe… punching people in the face is bad… put the brick down… there you go. No, NO! Back AWAY from that shovel… breathe… and smile. Poor Sensible Tracy. As if she doesn't have enough to do, she's run ragged trying to keep the homicidal urges in check. Note to self: Sensible Tracy needs to get laid. Investigate options.

Every girl plays the "what if" game at some time in her innocent (or not) adolescence. Usually at pyjama parties with other giggly teenagers, or in shocked, gossipy whispers after hearing of some other Unfortunate Girl in Trouble. Can't you just hear those capital letters clanging into place? What would I do? Long before I ever even met David, I thought I knew. Before it actually happened to me, my friends and I thought we had it worked out. One said she'd have an abortion, one chose adoption and Cathy said she'd go away to have the baby, then pass it off as her mother's child. A bit loopy, that one. She'd definitely read too many romance novels, and she was very worried about her family's standing in the community. If I remember correctly, where her family stood was mostly on the brink of divorce, bankruptcy and psychological collapse. Go figure.

The consensus was that our boyfriends would dump us, our parents would kill us and our lives would be over, the last two being entirely separate issues, in case you were wondering. You can always count on middle-school girls for drama and great lashings of hot air. We all said these things, but how many of us really thought about what they meant? We were all adamant that we knew what we'd do. We were young, and it wasn't something any of us were seriously considering (although, God knows, there were those who should've been. I wasn't the only hussy in the bunch, I'll have you know), because we all knew in our hearts it would never happen to us. We were all way too clever, way too good. We weren't like those Other Girls. We had the theory sorted, and that was all we needed. Smug? Well, of course, yes.

But then reality jumps you in the alley, knees you in the groin and head-butts you in the face, and smugness gets swallowed along with your teeth. It's different when it's real. It's different when it's you. "What am I going to do?" is much harder to answer than "what would I do?" Can you ever really decide something as huge as this without it having happened to you? I don't think so.

At first I tried to figure it out the Sensible Way. I was confusing The Decision with The Plan. I didn't know they were completely different things. I thought you made The Decision with a list, bullet-points and checkboxes, eliminating the impossible until you're left with a solution. But that's where I was wrong. The Decision comes straight from the universe into your soul, bypassing the brain entirely. It's a tiny thing, so you don't notice when it wriggles under your skin and makes its way to the centre of you. Small and unsure at first, it grows stronger every day until it's loud enough for you to hear. And then you realise you'd known all along.

Sensible Tracy couldn't understand this. These feeble notions of destiny and souls just irritated her. She was all about the numbers. Pros and cons of each option, colour-coded and graded according to probability of success. She was so proud of that list, I didn't have the heart to tell her to bugger off.

Sensible has lists for absolutely everything in my life: lists for work, lists for home, lists of life goals, lists of cheesecake ingredients, lists of lists, and her favourite: ***The List of Every Bad Thing I've Ever Done In My Life***. It's a long list, updated virtually daily.

Sensible Tracy brings out The List whenever I'm feeling down – just to remind me that anything I might be unhappy about is probably my fault. She's added a handy search function for user-friendliness, and can locate any Bad Thing in less than three seconds, no matter the magnitude or point in history. It can be sorted alphabetically, chronologically or by category of fuck-up. She's sensible, but I didn't say she was sane. There's got to be ***someone*** she can shag?

Naturally, she made a list of her options:

Sensible Tracy's List of Options For The Hopelessly Pregnant Teenager (including panel discussion)

Adoption? No, no. Definitely not going to happen. Why? Don't know. It may have seemed like the logical choice. There was a time (for about five minutes), just before confirmation of the pregnancy, when David and I had discussed adoption. We had "decided" it was the only option. He hugged me and we cried together. We said things like, "it's for the best", and "it's the only way". The relief was plain on his face and it made me sad. That look of last-minute reprieve in his eyes was probably the reason I went to the hospital by myself. It was the first sign that I'd be doing this alone, no matter what was decided.

Although I had agreed to it, I was aware that adoption wasn't my real choice. It was still one of those adolescent, pretend, "What If" decisions, and I knew it would change. Still, it was something to say when no other words sounded right. So we said it.

Abortion? No, again. Firstly, it was still illegal in those days, so it was never referred to directly. It was called "Doing Something". You'd have to find a doctor willing to Do Something, without telling him exactly what it was you wanted him To Do. And it just felt wrong. I clutched my belly protectively whenever someone mentioned it, even before I had much belly to clutch.

I don't think I was being dramatic; I wasn't taking a brave moral stand or anything. I understood that for some people, sometimes, it's the choice they have to make. I just didn't think that I was one of those people, or that this was one of those times.

Surely there had to be other choices?

Another list, I'm afraid.

Sensible Tracy's Sub-List of Options For Keeping The Baby

Have the baby and marry David
Have the baby and hand him over to my parents to raise
Have the baby and raise him myself, with help and support from my parents

Let's review.

Option number one: Do I ***look*** stupid to you? Don't answer that. Believe it or not, there were people who thought we should get married. I could understand if the suggestion had been offered only by silly children my own age, but it wasn't. There were some perfectly sane looking adults wandering around, who assumed I'd be waddling down the aisle before the year was out.

Can you believe the things people come up with? Up until then, I'd always believed that adults knew better. I thought they were in charge and could be relied upon to do the right thing and give the right advice. I was flabbergasted to discover that while some adults are reasonably intelligent and doing their best, there are equally many who are completely fucking bonkers. And you can't tell just by looking at them. Disguised as normal people, like teachers or kindly old ladies in Shoprite, these nutjobs wield immense authority over the lives and choices of innocent young people too dumb to know better. And the poor kiddies never know that the citizens in charge are smoking their socks. What a scary thought. It makes you wonder just who exactly is driving the bus here? I mean, really. To get married at my age to someone I barely knew, let's face it – and bring a child into such a dodgy situation? Good grief. That's a whole episode of Ricki Lake all by itself. Marriage for the right reasons is hard enough, but for the wrong ones? That's just madness. At least I knew that.

So, no. There would be no tinkly sound of wedding bells or shotguns in my immediate future. Of course, I didn't know then that there'd be no wedding bells in my distant future either. But that's a fish of a different kidney altogether.

Option number two: right, so I would carry the baby for nine months, give birth, hold him in my arms – and then dump him with my mother and carry on with my life? Leave my parents to love him, feed him, comfort him, raise him? Live in the same house as my baby, with me a stranger or sister? Go back to the way things were before, with school, boys and attempted suicide? Let a child of my body, my heart, grow up seeing his mother every day, and knowing she doesn't care enough to ***be*** a mother? Who does stuff like that?

Not me, that's for damn sure. No, it seemed like motherhood was the only choice. Real motherhood: Option Three. If I was going to do this, I would have to do it right.

It's all very well deciding this in your head. It's quite another convincing others that you haven't taken leave of your senses. I was dreading telling my mother what I'd decided. I was expecting arguments, threats and general motherly bullying. I wasn't sure if I could stand up to that. I thought I'd give in and let her tell me what to do. Yet I didn't know how I'd live with myself if I did that.

But my mother didn't argue. She didn't threaten or bully. My mother did a brave thing. She left it up to me. She trusted me enough to make the choice myself. That's because she was cleverer than me.

Sitting on the lawn behind the garage that afternoon, she asked warily, "So, what do you want to do?"

I panicked for a second, because I hadn't done my bar-graphs yet. Then I looked in her eyes and I realised she didn't want graphs. I knew she was still cross with me, but I could see that she didn't hate me, either. She never had. She was just scared for me.

"I want to keep the baby. I'm going to keep the baby." It was weird to hear the words said out loud. It was weird that it was me saying them. I really did want this, more than anything else in the world. Even weirder was the realisation that I would fight for it, no matter what I had to do. ***No matter what.*** That was my first maternal thought, and it's one every mother recognises. I think my own mother saw it in me.

Then I began to cry (big surprise).

"But I don't know how I'm going to do it!"

I was scared because I knew I had no plan, five-minute, five-year, or any kind of a plan at all. I was graphless. All I had was the little voice in my head. I'd thought Mom would say I couldn't keep the baby, that it wouldn't work. "Over my dead body," I expected her to say. "You're on your own." The Ugly Cry loomed.

But I'd underestimated my mother, as children do. She just loved me and was doing her best, making it up as she went along.

She put her arms around me and said, "Okay. Okay. That's what we'll do." Her voice wobbled, but she held me and didn't let go for a long time. She knew The Decision was something I had to make by myself. The Plan, on the other hand, we could do together. I told you she was clever.

Eventually we stood up to go inside. I was shaky on my feet, my legs all pins and needles, and desperate for the toilet again. I was a queasy and tearful mess. So it is peculiar that it should hit me then, in that state – I was no longer a child. I was a grown-up now, a mother. Me. Who'd have thunk it?

I'd never felt like that before, that determined and that terrified. I didn't know I had it in me to feel so strongly, to feel so ***strong*** and so utterly fragile at the same time. I was afraid, but I wasn't lost any more. For the first time in my life there wasn't a black hole where my future should have been. The road ahead was fuzzy and I knew it would be hard, but it was there. That's a big deal.

Sensible Tracy's list of every bad thing I've ever done in my life: Abridged and censored

- Accidentally letting sweet wrapper blow away in the wind; didn't try very hard to catch it
- Allowing learner's licence to expire three times and still not having driver's licence
- Eating entire (huge) packet of ***Flings*** and blaming it on the dog (more than once)
- Chasing after boyfriend's car in the street, after he left in a huff
- Cheating on boyfriend (different one)
- Neglecting to save ant found half-drowned in the bath
- Getting atrociously drunk at friend's twenty-first, and having to be brought home in disgrace by said friend's mother
- Forgetting to complete company attendance register, telling boss book had been water-damaged by leaking roof, necessitating its having to be thrown away
- Having two children by two different fathers and displaying alarming lack of shame for imprudence
- Hanging up on telesales consultant
- Letting child go two nights in a row without bathing
- Pushing mother off bed while play-fighting, necessitating X-rays of leg and crazy volumes of

bandages (bad one, this – years later Mom's leg still hurts in cold weather, even if she says it doesn't)

- Eating polony sandwich before class had finished saying grace in preschool at age four
- Telling kindly beggar I had no money; later finding unexpected R5 in pocket, spending it on sweets
- Writing name on black dustbin at school in Grade Two

There's lots of other stuff. Some of it's not so bad. Lots of it I'll never tell.

Chapter Three

1993: ***In which she cries over the spilt beans that thicken the plot***

The Plan began to take shape over the next few weeks. The biggest worry was my education. The idea was that I'd get through the year, then do Grade Ten by correspondence the following. After the birth, I'd take a short break, then I'd work in the mornings while my mom babysat. That seemed a sensible arrangement.

The only catch was finishing that year. It was still only August. By December, I'd be five months pregnant and definitely showing. My parents were terrified that if the school found out, they'd make me leave immediately. If I left with four months left of Grade Nine, I'd probably never catch up. I didn't want to fall behind and end up giving up on my education altogether. If I couldn't finish this year, I'd have to go back to a different school after the baby was born and repeat the year – that is, if I could find a school that would take me. And I did not want to go back to school again. That was just the worst idea imaginable. I couldn't bear the thought of hanging out with all those giggly girlies, pretending to be interested in their nail polish dilemmas when all I wanted was to be with my child. I wasn't afraid of gossip or judgement (okay, I was a little), but I was afraid I'd lose it and push someone down the stairs if I heard another word about What My Boyfriend Said To The Chick Who Called Me A Slag On Saturday Night Outside The Vic… And the idea of class netball and demerits and “abstinence first” lectures just made me want to snigger, or hurl. Or both.

And so began the Great Belly-Hiding Conspiracy. I ***did*** get a really big jersey. I pretended to have a dreadful and protracted case of salmonella. I told the physical ed teacher I couldn’t do gymnastics because I had a bad chest. My incredible craving for grotty tuck shop Cornish pasties and Liquaroos was dismissed as a passing teenage fad. My bizarre emotional outbursts could have been anything, really. I was a fourteen-year-old girl; emotional outbursts are mandatory.

All would have been fine, really, if only I’d kept my fucking mouth shut. But could I do that? No, of course not. I was a teenager, after all. And what do teenage girls do? Besides giggling and self-consciously smoking Benson and Hedges Special Mild without inhaling? They ***talk,*** of course. To other teenage girls.

I told all my friends. Shortly after the pregnancy was confirmed (like, the very next day), I convened a Council of War in the girls’ bathroom.

My announcement was greeted with much screeching and hugging and profanity. One of them told me how wonderful and exciting it all was. I mean, sure, it was – at least, it would be once we got past the bit that was impossibly scary. Even though it was unfair of me to expect them to understand, or be cross with them because they didn’t, I still wanted to smack her cheerful little face.

I asked them not to tell anybody. That really meant nobody – not their boyfriends, parents or random classmates on the bus. I explained that if the Governing Body found out, they would probably expel me and then my chances of ever finishing school would be virtually zero. This wasn't a little secret like someone bunking or someone kissing someone else's boyfriend. It was huge. It was real. Serious shit. I was trusting them with my whole life – my future and the future of my child. They were my best friends and I thought I could. And like the good friends they were, they swore blind they'd never tell anybody. I believed them.

But, like me, they did what girls do, and within weeks everybody at school knew. I don't know how many blabbed, but one person would probably have been enough. People began to whisper and stare at my tummy as I passed, but I tried to ignore them. I counted the days until the end of the year and read my booklet a lot.

As the weeks went by, I took to hiding behind desks and handy trees whenever a teacher got too close. In particular, I avoided Dragon Lady, the Chairlady of the School Governing Body and God, as far as our little town was concerned. She was a prominent elderly citizen with her fingers in more pies than a New Jersey Mafioso. She lurked around the school often, planting flowers in the quad and reading prayers at assemblies. She scared the hell out of me, with her daffy gardening hat and little green trowel. She looked so benign; you'd never guess she ate Bad Girls for breakfast. I imagined she'd toss me out of school in a second if she knew. She'd make an example of me, the ghastly affront to the fine, upstanding morals and good name of the school that I was.

She may well have been just a sweet old lady doing her bit for the community. Who knows? I could have had it wrong. That was my year for misjudging people.

In the end, it was neither my loose-lipped friends, nor a suspicious old biddy who caught me out. It was yours truly who, single-handedly, brought to light the Great Conspiracy. And in spectacular fashion, too, on my fifteenth birthday. An event full of high drama, with dustbins and delicate sensibilities flying in all directions.

Before I was pregnant, I'd been counting the minutes until my fifteenth birthday. I'd always loved birthdays – loved the presents and the fuss of my own, special day. This birthday, in particular, seemed important. Secretly, I believed turning fifteen would change my life – I'd be one step closer to that impossibly magical number of sixteen, and finally over the misery that was fourteen. Fifteen-year-old me would be someone new – a girl with confidence and grace, one who could talk to anyone, or catch a stranger's eye and make him wonder about me. A sexy, personal theme tune would play as I sashayed down the street, all eyes fixed on me. Beefy, white-t-shirted mechanics and young hotties in generic sailors' uniforms would turn to stare as one, movements fluidly synchronised and choreographed.

At fourteen, you simply cannot be that girl, no matter how often you shave your legs. Eyeliner doesn't help, either. I didn't understand that the number made no difference. Confidence and grace take a long, long time to come (personally, I'm still waiting), and no amount of Max Factor Smoky Kohl will make them pitch up faster. Mothers have been trying to pass down this profound Zen wisdom to their daughters for untold generations; unfortunately, their scantily-clad daughters steadfastly continue to disbelieve them. They're too busy rolling their smudgy, raccoon eyes.

So, I'd thought turning fifteen was a big deal. Of course, that was ***before.*** Pregnancy changed all that. September 6th started like any other day in many a first trimester: random gagging, followed by an intimate conversation with the loo and topped off with a small, redundant ginger biscuit for nausea. Which doesn't work, by the way, in case you wondered. Still, a cookie's a cookie and not to be sniffed at.

My family gave me presents that morning, as they'd always done, but it wasn't the same. There was none of the excitement and goofy ***aw-shucks***-ness that came with previous birthdays. It was all a bit of a let-down, even though I got the Revlon make-up I'd asked for ages ago. I suppose it was my first adult birthday – the one where you realise you're not so important after all and the world doesn't actually give a rat's ass about your cake. No more Special Treatment for the Birthday Girl when you're a grown-up. No gold star, no silver tiara. Just another day of scrubbing the toilet and taking out the rubbish. Or telling your teacher you're pregnant. As the case may be.

Besides the whole issue of Being-Pregnant-At-Fourteen-Slash-Fifteen – rather a big issue, in anyone's book – I was also dealing with rampaging pregnancy hormones. I was prone to sudden, irrational crying jags that could last for hours and send friends, family and little dogs diving for cover. I was impatient and sometimes cruel. I hated everybody and everything, and all I wanted to do was sleep, puke and eat cookies. A textbook case, in other words.

They say knowing you're normal makes you feel better – I say ***PUH!*** Until you're at least four months pregnant, normal doesn't exist. You ***know*** you're crazy and you ***know*** that no-one else in the history of baby-making has ever felt as crap as you do right now. And you really don't care to be told that everything you're feeling is perfectly natural and will pass soon enough. ***Of course*** you're going to be a retching, oozing blimp for the rest of your life.

It was in this unstable frame of mind that I set off for school, even though the thought of smelly science labs made my head hurt. I gritted my teeth and tried to swallow the fits of rage that kept popping up whenever anyone said "happy birthday".

I sat glowering and muttering grumpily to myself at the group table in class. The first period of the day was S.U.R.E. – Silent Uninterrupted Reading for Enjoyment, that is. Otherwise known as Sundry Unfulfilled Randiness for Everybody, depending on the time of the month and the table at which you were sitting. Busy, busy pheromones; no rest for the horny. Except for me, obviously. I couldn't get within ten metres of a pheromone without feeling queasy.

Ms H was the most feared person in the school (except for the janitor, a mean, Jelly Tot-shaped man who wore nasty, grubby white lab coats over teeny little shorts, and Joey, the ghost in the Home Ec corridor). She had terrorised generations of unruly teenagers, her luridly dyed, reddish-purple hair and yellow suits the stuff of legend. Do not tangle with Ms H when she's wearing yellow. It was a chicken or the egg thing, I don't know which came first – the migraine-inducing outfit or the vicious mood. Either way, it was one of those things everybody knew. I want to say she was wearing yellow that day, but I can't be sure.

I don't know who it was, but ***somebody*** set her off. She must have thought someone at our table was chatting, that cardinal sin of the schoolroom, a transgression far worse than talking. Maybe someone had been, but it wasn't us. We were reading innocently. Which is why I was so astonished when she lost it. Maybe she was contending with hormonal issues of her own. Whatever the reason, she descended on us like a purple-haired Aztec monster goddess. Eyes bulging, neck veins popping, bosoms swinging wildly from side to side. Ms H was furious.

"I don't know what to do with you lot! There's just no respect! You think you can do as you please! If you want to chat, you'd better get out and do it somewhere else!" she shouted. She ranted and raved for at least five minutes, arms waving and spit flying. It was totally unfair. We were hardly the "problem kids"; we were all reasonably well-behaved and could be relied upon not to start any fires or smoke dope in class.

Under normal circumstances, I'd probably have sat there blushing and trying not to cry, waiting for the floor to open up and swallow me. But normal circumstances these were not. My blood began to boil. There's really no better way to describe it. As I was getting angrier and angrier, holding my breath and biting my tongue, my bum involuntarily clenching the seat, it felt as if my blood was progressively heating up to a gentle simmer, then to a brisk boil until it became an aggressive, red-hot throb under my skin, my head pounding apace, as I fumed at the crazy injustice of it all. I'd never been so damn mad in all my life. I wanted to jump up and tell her to stop being such a loony. I wanted to punch her on the nose. I didn't for a minute imagine myself doing it, though. Of course not. Good Girls Do Not Shout At People In Authority. But, wooh boy, was I wrong. They ***do.*** Sometimes they do worse. And when Good Girls Disobey, you had better bloody well get out of the way.

I was having a really crap day – it was my birthday, I was pregnant, nauseous, scared and angry. And here comes a mad woman accusing me of something I hadn't done. I'd had enough. If this were a cartoon, my face would've been bright red and steam would have been billowing out of my ears.

Suddenly my clenched bum gave up its valiant struggle – it could keep me on my seat no longer. I shot to my feet, stumbling away a few paces. Ms H stopped in mid-harangue, stunned into silence. She couldn't believe what she was seeing. The whole class sat enthralled: this was good stuff. The mousy little girl nobody ever noticed was about to get herself into some deep shit and they were fascinated.

I stood at the table, shocked that I'd even gone this far. ***Oooh crap, what the hell now?*** I couldn't very well sit down again. That would look stupid. Besides, I was still angry. Wild-eyed, I was running on adrenaline now and not thinking straight at all. Sensible Tracy was cowering in a corner somewhere, gibbering and terrified. ***She*** was no help.

"And where do you think you're going?" Ms H asked. She had recovered enough composure to rustle up some face-saving sarcasm. She truly thought I'd surrender, but we were both horrified to discover that this was not going to happen.

"I'm … I'm … I'm going out! I'm leaving!" I declared, all overblown bluster and pretend confidence. The high-noon moment ticked away as we stood staring each other down, eyes narrowed and fingers twitching. The class sat breathless: who would fold first? As the adrenaline and anger drained away, it left only dismay and terminal embarrassment. I had to get out of there before I burst into tears. I started towards the door.

"You're not going anywhere, young lady! Get back here this instant!" yelled Ms H, nostrils flaring and panic rising. Clearly, this wasn't how it was supposed to go. I ignored her this time – if I'd tried to talk, I would've cracked. I swept out of the class in what I hoped was dramatic fashion, tripping over a small wastepaper basket and nearly breaking an ankle. As I slammed the door behind me, the nausea and flashy lights started. I almost passed out then, but I staggered into the library and sat down to catch my breath. I skulked in the teen fiction section for two hours before anybody found me.

Ms H didn't drag me to the principal demanding a public hanging for gross insubordination. Oh no, it was far worse than that. She sat me down in her office (a grand name for the printing room, a dusty cavern with ancient printing machines lurking threateningly in the corner) and flicked the Concerned Mentor switch.

"Tell me, Tracy. There must be something going on. This isn't like you..." She was actually being kind, or at least trying. I was silent, sullen, miserable. I wouldn't tell her, I ***wouldn't.*** If I blabbed now, it would spoil everything. It would all be over. They'd send me away and our Plan would be ruined.

I tried to hold onto my anger, hoping it would keep my mouth shut. I thought she was trying to trick me, acting concerned so I'd spill my guts all over her yellow shoes (they ***were*** yellow! I remember now! So she must have been wearing her yellow suit that day, after all! I ***knew*** it!)

She started guessing.

"Is everything All Right At Home? Are your parents getting divorced?" I shook my head. Good grief.

"Are you eating properly? You haven't been starving yourself have you? You know, you girls and your diets, I just don't understand it."

Jay-zus woman! Do I look like a freaking anorexic to you? I nearly laughed at that one, but just shook my head again. It was the Spanish Inquisition without the instruments of torture, although I was beginning to wonder about those printing machines.

She ran down the list of Society's Ills, trying to get me to admit to something. Abusive parents, drugs, depression, bulimia – everything except pregnancy. I don't know why she didn't think of it. Perhaps, like everyone else, she couldn't quite believe that Dreary Virginal Tracy had ever been within spitting distance of a boy.

I was starting to lose it. Somewhere around, "Are You Trapped In A Polygamous Religious Cult?", my strained self-control snapped and shot across the room like a cheap elastic band. ***Twang!*** I'd tried so hard to keep quiet, but she was like a Jack Russell with a bone and I was no match for her.

"No! No! It's nothing like that! I'm pregnant!" I barked. Shock. Horror. Damn.

She opened and closed her mouth a few times, looking just like a goldfish. A yellow goldfish with purple hair. Sputter, gasp, dribble. "Are you sure? At your age, your menstrual cycle hasn't settled down yet, you know. And these terrible crash diets can disrupt your periods too. Yes, ***yes***, that ***must*** be it."

Jeez, she wasn't letting go of this anorexia thing. I hadn't been skinny to start with and at nine weeks I wasn't huge, but nobody would be confusing me with Kate Moss any time soon. She was clutching at straws, a little frantic, trying to convince herself it was all a big mistake. I really did not have time for this. I spoke patiently and calmly, though I still felt like punching her in the nose.

"No ma'am, I'm sure. I've been to the doctor already. It's been confirmed; I'm about nine weeks now."

Panic gave way to haughty indignation. When all else fails, bully someone…

"What about your parents?" she snapped. "Where are they in all this? Did they not love you enough that you had to look for love with this… this … ***boy***?"

How rude!

"No! My parents love me! It's not their fault. They didn't do anything wrong!" I heard that childish shrillness in my voice again, but I couldn't help it, she was beginning to annoy me. She could think what she liked about me, but I wasn't having any interfering old bag disparage my parents, who had always done their best for us and were at no stage to blame for my misdemeanours.

Ms H was having none of it. Her middle-school psychology seminars were quite clear on the matter. It was all down to not enough love, not enough discipline, not enough boundaries, not enough green, leafy vegetables.

The cross-examination continued while I wondered where my next cookie was coming from. I felt sorry for her, eventually. She seemed bewildered, desperately scrabbling for some shred of sanity in a world gone mad. She'd never expected this of me, she told me. I had so much potential, she told me. I could have done so much better. She wanted to know where it had all gone wrong. Surely there must have been one traumatic, defining moment that had plunged me into this harrowing, downward spiral of degradation and self-destruction (big on psychology, even bigger on big words, Ms H). Repressed childhood abuse, perhaps? Unresolved weaning issues? Absent father, domineering mother? Surely there must have been something?

I tried to tell her it wasn't that complicated, but she wouldn't hear me. I didn't dare mention my Destiny and Providence theory. Nor the other popular hypothesis, the one where Shit Happens. I don't think either would have gone down well. She leaped from one wild conclusion to the next, and I waited until she was ready to listen. I fantasised about ginger biscuits and calculated the distance to the nearest toilet. Recent experience had taught me that it's best not to say too much at times like these. Best just to nod sagely with a suitably contrite expression, and let her get things off her chest. Rational thinking would return in a while, but for now it was all bluster and reproach. That was okay. I was familiar with the procedure.

She eventually ran out of steam, as I'd known she would, and then I told her about The Plan. I told her I was planning to keep the baby, finish my schooling by correspondence and be a good mother. I told her that my parents were supporting me and we were going to be okay. It sounded real when I said it, it sounded like it could really work. It was a good plan. She seemed impressed that we'd managed to get this far without her.

Then I broached the subject I'd been dreading.

"Ma'am," I began. "I … um … are you going to tell the principal? I know I'll have to leave then. Please, please, if you could just let me finish this year, I promise I won't be a problem. I really have to finish. Please don't tell him."

Then I cried again. I was exhausted. Stress, hormones and the strain of acting as if everything was normal had wiped me out completely. My body was tired, my mind was tired. I just wanted to go back to bed and sleep until April. Now, on top of everything else, it looked as if I might have to quit school – all because I couldn't keep my mouth shut for three lousy months. What jolly good fun.

Then scary Ms H did the unexpected. She hugged me. I could hardly believe it. Ms H was human, after all.

"You know, you remind me so much of my daughter. She was just as stubborn as you," she said vaguely as she wiped my eyes. This may or may not have been a compliment. I didn't know how to take it.

"You know I have to tell the principal," she continued. "But I'm sure he'll be reasonable. I'm sure we can work something out for you. Don't worry; it'll be fine, you'll see."

Another hug, my head still reeling from the first. You learn something new every day. Imagine learning that Ms H was really quite sweet. Our relationship changed overnight – we weren't just teacher and pupil anymore, we became something like equals. It was good to have someone to talk to, someone who was genuinely interested and not just for the gossip value. She became my friend.

Much to the disappointment of my class mates, who were hoping for more live-action cat fighting, I was allowed to go home after our talk. When I phoned my mom to fetch me, I had to admit the jig was up. She was not pleased. I didn't know it was possible for her to be more pissed off with me than she already was, but she found a way.

My future – and my baby's – was now in the hands of cranky bureaucratic fogies who didn't know me, and whose main concern would be What People Would Say. Another sleepless night.

Mr C was an intimidating man – tall and not very friendly-looking. Maybe he just had a naturally angry face. My mother and I had been summoned to his office and I was nervous. I'd never been in there before. Ms H had said I needn't worry, but I was still wary. After all, this was the man who, the year before, had written a scathing letter to all the parents, exposing their children's sordid shenanigans at all-night beach parties, during which drinking and fornication in the bushes had been the order of the day. Nobody ever asked how he knew what went on in the bushes, and perhaps it was better that way. And yes, he really did use the word fornication. I hardly expected him to be agreeable to letting me swan around school for the next three months with my growing belly and unpredictable mood swings.

I thought I was in for a lecture on Standards and the School's Good Name and Setting An Example, but it wasn't forthcoming. Instead, Mr C asked what I was going to do. He asked about continuing my education and who would look after the baby, but he didn't make us feel bad. He could have – we were expecting it and I thought I deserved it – but it didn't come. Again, I was surprised to find that this forbidding man was just a person like me, muddling through life and doing his best. More and more, I was learning that adults were not the all-knowing, all-powerful supreme beings I'd thought they were. This was a confusing discovery. I didn't know whether it made me feel better or worse.

Mr C said I could finish the year and write my December exams, but I had to make sure the Governing Body (Mafia Gardening Lady and her tea-drinking cronies) didn't find out, because they might not be so accommodating. They had to think of official visits from education department inspectors and government funding and stuff like that – they wouldn't want a pregnant girl wandering around brazenly on the school grounds, where she could be a bad influence on anyone.

He asked who knew about the pregnancy, and I fudged the details a little, I'm afraid. I couldn't admit that everybody south of Cavendish Square probably knew by now. Well-known scientific fact: the closest thing to the speed of light is the speed of gossip in a suburban middle school. It was surprising that the teachers hadn't heard this juicy piece of scandal. Of course, I said I'd only told one or two close friends and they would keep quiet. I just prayed that some nasty kid wouldn't tell the head honchos, just for fun. I imagined certain other parents finding out; the outrage and uproar and emergency PTA meetings, the mob of angry pitchfork-wielding villagers baying for my blood.

I'd expected it to be much harder than this. I'd prepared myself for expulsion. I was getting used to the idea of a life spent waitressing. I hadn't expected sympathy and simple kindness from anybody at all, let alone my teachers. I kept looking for the pitchforks, but so far there were none. Ms H didn't have to grill me for answers; she could have given me detention instead and thought nothing of it. She didn't have to speak to the principal on my behalf. And he didn't have to let me stay. None of them had to help me. None of them had to care at all, and yet they did. If they hadn't, my life might have been very different.

***

And so life went on. You wouldn't think it could, but it did. I still went to school every day, I still went out with my friends, although this was becoming increasingly awkward. We were starting to drift apart, and I suppose that's normal. Sometimes I found it hard to accept that things were changing between us, and sometimes I felt quite alone, even when I was with them. I know I wasn't a very good friend during this time – my mood swings and self-absorption must have seemed bizarre and maybe over-exaggerated to them.

Still, the sun came up every morning, and the weeks passed by as they always had. I planned, I daydreamed, I worried. I went to the doctor for monthly check-ups, the baby and I were both healthy. Things were going according to plan, mostly. We still had bad days sometimes, but things were moving on.

One morning, I woke up with a tingly, nervous feeling in my stomach. I couldn't place it for a minute. With a little shock, I realised it was excitement. I was excited to meet my child and to become a mother. I was excited about the future. It was a great feeling. Knowing that I was a proper mother with real maternal feelings, real love for my baby, and not a tragic planned parenthood poster child, me happy. It made me proud. I walked around with a silly grin on my face the whole day. Besides all the practical arrangements falling into place, now I knew that my baby would be safe with me. He would be loved. I wouldn't let him down.

Chapter Four

1994: *In which she chucks her man and finds her feet*

And so we come quite neatly to the subject of David, which I cannot avoid although I've been trying like hell to think of a way. It's hard to talk about, because those were difficult days and I know they weren't my most shining moments.

We must go back a few weeks to when I first found out. As I said, David wasn't with me when I found out I was pregnant. When I gave him the news over the phone, I told him I'd be breaking the news to my parents that night, and that he should do the same.

Soon after that, a meeting was arranged between his mother and my parents. We were all going to sit down together and discuss The Situation. Nobody was looking forward to it. Everybody was stressed out and distracted, and nobody was thinking clearly. It's no surprise, then, that things went so wrong that night. A comedy of errors, you might call it, if you were feeling jovial and didn't mind being coshed over the head with an ornamental table lamp.

What happened was this. You see, they thought we were meeting at ***our*** house, and we thought we were meeting at ***theirs.*** So while they were waiting in the car outside our house, we were waiting in the car outside theirs. Their house was in darkness, so obviously nobody was at home, unless they were hiding behind the couch. The thought did cross my mind. It soon became clear that they weren't coming back –nobody wanted to say it, but we were all thinking they'd made a duck. We drove home in silence. I sat in the back seat and entertained evil thoughts. I was furious with David. I thought he'd let me down on purpose, and I hated him for making me look stupid.

Imagine our embarrassment when we arrived home to find them sitting in their car outside our house. Somehow we'd gotten our wires crossed, each thinking the other lot were a bunch of inconsiderate twits, spineless jellyfish who couldn't or wouldn't keep a simple appointment. There was some awkward small talk about the amusing mistake, with fake-jolly comments along the lines of "Ho, ho, some miscommunication there, somewhere." And then much glaring at the other side because of course, ***we*** didn't miscommunicate anything – no, it must have been ***them.*** We ***said*** we'd meet at their place, you know. It was all arranged.

This sort of thing never happens in real life. Just as you're starting to think you had the date or time wrong, your friend or your train or your interviewer will saunter up nonchalantly as if you hadn't been waiting forty minutes at all. And you still don't know, do you, if they were late or you were early. And you never will. However, this time it did happen, and it happened in real life.

We all sat down in the lounge drinking the terrible, weak coffee I'd made, and the adults spoke about what was to be done. There was no overt unpleasantness, but if looks could kill, determining who dunnit would have proved a forensic challenge, what with all those tiny daggers sticking out of everybody's backs.

We spoke about The Plan and they said they'd do their bit. Dad said he wasn't concerned about What People Would Say, he and Mom just wanted the best for me. My father, the hero. I wonder whether he knows how proudly I remember this. It meant a lot to hear him say it. In the end, not much was resolved that night at all. It was just a preliminary meeting in a spirit of general politeness and saying the correct things. A meeting to discuss the possibility of future meetings.

Then they went home and we sat and drank more coffee and spoke about how that wasn't so bad, how it could have been worse, and aren't they a bunch of wallies for going to the wrong house? I'm quite sure they sat in their lounge saying exactly the same things about us. Comedy of errors, see?

So David and I were still together, after a fashion. I found myself increasingly irritated by him, by his crying and his need for support and direction and his "yes-man" personality. He said the things I wanted to hear, but with no idea of the implications. People have said he was too young; he wasn't ready for the responsibility. People have told me I shouldn't be too hard on him.

Fine, then. Maybe he wasn't ready and maybe he ***was*** too young. But how does that explain me? I was four years younger and I was doing okay. As scared as I was, I was taking responsibility for my child and our future. If I could do it, surely so could he? But, then again, I do have that mule-headed resolve you can bounce rocks off. Maybe I ***was*** expecting too much from him. I don't know. I just don't have an answer for that one.

Our relationship hobbled along on two broken legs for a few more weeks, but I knew it wouldn't last. I needed support, somebody to lean on, and I knew he couldn't give me that. We broke up. It was difficult and I felt guilty and mean. Hormones being the way they were, I may have been a bit nasty to him. Everybody seemed to think I was punishing him. He may have thought so, too. My friends were angry with me for breaking up with him. They thought I was cruel and unfair. But I still think it was the only thing I could have done.

We didn't see each other for a long time after that. After a month or two, I heard that he'd started dating one of my friends. I was hurt. Not because I wanted him for myself, but because he seemed to be carrying on with his life as if nothing had happened. As if he didn't have a child coming into the world, one who would need his love and care and protection. As if the tiny baby I already loved so fiercely didn't exist. I was also hurt because I seemed to be the last to know. Everybody else had known for ages and had hidden it from me, maybe to keep me from getting upset. I felt very alone when I found out, as if I'd been left behind while everyone else moved on, relieved that I wasn't their problem anymore.

David dating his new girlfriend really threw me. It came at a time that I'd just begun to find my feet again. As the second trimester approached, my body and my mind began to return to normal and I was becoming less unpredictably emotional. I was now looking to the future and I could see it wouldn't be so bad.

But faced with a new emotional upheaval, I lost myself for a little while, there. The strain of not fitting in with ***anybody*** anymore overtook me. I might have been depressed, actually. I'd be fine at home, but as soon as I walked onto the school grounds, I'd turn morose, bitchy or tearful. Sometimes all at once.

I remember having a photo taken on the night of the Grade Nine dance. I must have been about twelve weeks then. We were all dressed up, the girls in beautiful dresses and the boys in suits. It was a big night for most of us, and I'd been looking forward to it for a long time. But it was terrible. The difference between ***me*** and ***them*** had never been clearer. I wandered around alone most of the time, biting the head off anyone who dared speak to me. I shouldn't have gone at all. I should have stayed at home and repacked my baby clothes instead. That always made me feel better.

When I saw the photo later, I was shocked. All the others looked so happy, so full of enthusiasm and promise. I just looked miserable, like a girl who had nothing good in her life, one who couldn't see anything good in the future, either.

I didn't want to be that person. After the dance, I tried hard to be positive at school. I tried not to take offence at people's unthinking, insensitive comments. I tried to tell myself it was almost over – just a couple of months, then I'd be free. I'd be able to leave all that behind and get on with my real life.

I first felt my baby kick as I wrote my final Science exam. I sat in the exam room trying to remember the difference between a pipette and a burette, when I felt a funny little butterfly-twinge kind of flutter in my stomach. I dropped my pencil.

Could it be? Nah – surely not. Is that how it's supposed to feel? I don't know… but that felt strange. I sat still for ages, hoping it would come again, and just as I'd decided it was my gristly Cornish pasty coming back to haunt me, I felt it again.

This time, there was no mistaking it. My little baby was kicking. He was kicking!

The happiness I felt – well, you can't really describe it. Feeling that kick meant so many things. It meant he was healthy and on schedule. It meant this was all ***real.*** And I think he was telling me to hold on. He wanted me to know this horrible school ordeal was almost over, and then we'd be together.

I couldn't concentrate properly on the exam after that, but I did okay. I now had a little angel looking out for me. My job was to look after ***him,*** and that meant not giving in to despondency or loneliness.

I was ready.

***

The end of that school year was one of the happiest days of my life. I walked out of the gates on the last day and never looked back, not even once. I didn't see much of my friends over summer, but that was okay. I was just happy to be home with my family, preparing my study routine, finding my way around my new life and making a place in the world for my baby. I suspect I may have been all glowy. Fat, but glowy. Unable to get up out of armchairs on my own, but quite radiant.

I spent hours packing and rearranging baby clothes, trying to imagine the person who'd soon be wearing them. I couldn't picture what he would look like and my image of him changed every day. Sometimes I thought he was a girl, sometimes I was convinced he was a boy, sometimes with blonde hair, sometimes brown. I dreamed of him too, but I could never see his face properly. The only thing I was sure of was that his eyes would be blue. And they were. If it was a boy, his name would be Ethan. If it was a girl, it would be Britney. Yes, yes, may the God of Ridiculous, Skanky Names strike me down where I stand. Ethan is acceptable, but dear Lord, I confess there will never be any excuse for Britney. In my defence, Britney Spears had not yet been invented – at least there's that.

Most of my baby things were second-hand, given to me by friends of aunts and aunts of friends, some of whom I'd never even met. I was surprised by how many people were willing to help, I suspect because they felt sorry for me. That bugged me, because I certainly didn't feel I needed to be pitied. However, since beggars cannot be choosers, if there was free stuff in it for me, I'd make the effort to look a little tragic. A single, silent tear, a bravely quivering lip, a well-timed shoulder-heaving sigh here and there… People like that sort of thing. It's expected. Just joking!

Really – I was grateful for all the help and care I received from friends, family and perfect strangers. I didn't mind second-hand. People had shared with me out of love and generosity (and maybe a little smug superiority at times, but I can't prove it), so what did it matter if some things were a bit old or faded?

The second-hand cot was all set up and awaiting its little passenger. I was so proud of all this paraphernalia. Other moms will understand. It made everything seem more real somehow, even though I still struggled to get my head around the idea sometimes. I'd be getting dressed or shopping or having a shower and suddenly it would hit me that a real little person was in there, a real little person getting ready to come out, to meet the world and check out what kind of mother he'd been saddled with.

I had moments of terror, times when I was paralysed by the thought that there had been a terrible mistake. Whatever gave me the idea that I could be trusted with the life of another human being? Clearly, when they sent this poor child to be looked after by me, somebody up there wasn't doing their job – I couldn't even put a nappy on straight, though I'd been practising on dolls for months. I had absolutely no idea what I was doing. I'd read all the books, but I still didn't believe I'd be able to figure any of it out once it all became real. I knew, ***just bloody knew,*** that I'd be the only mother in the history of the world who'd never figure out which end of the baby was up. Sooner or later, the administrative error would be noticed and corrected, and somebody in authority would swoop down and whisk my poor child off to his proper parents, saving him from a lifetime of saggy nappies and parental idiocy.

I had many such What-The-Hell-Was-I-Thinking moments, but I found obsessive-compulsive reorganising of baby toiletries most beneficial and calming. I'm convinced they put some kind of mood-altering substance in Elizabeth Anne's baby shampoo – it always made me feel better, no matter how low I was. I know I can't be the only mother-to-be to sniff enough of it to pass out.

I craved smells rather than food. Besides my Elizabeth Anne's snorting habit, I also developed a thing for the nostril-melting aroma of subway disinfectant. Hey, some women like pickles and ice-cream – I liked Jeyes Fluid. Nothing wrong with that, is there?

Besides the second-hand goodies, I did have a brand new pram – my pride and joy. My granny bought it. She'd bought the prams for most of her grandchildren, and now she did the same for her first great-grandchild. To be included in her personal little tradition made me happy – I felt like we belonged, my baby and I.

Shopping for the Right Pram is a time-consuming business, but after hours of searching, we eventually found just the thing. I spotted it in a tiny baby shop and I wanted it immediately. It may just as well have drifted down to me on a radiant, gossamer cloud to the glorious accompaniment of angel song. Oh, it was beautiful. It was a dark-green Posh Baby pram with splashes of cerise pink and buttery yellow. Very nineties. Of course, these days Posh Baby is not so posh anymore – it doesn't sound nearly Italian enough, and, not being tastefully understated in khaki or navy blue, completely fails in the modern elegance department. But back then, I loved my Poshie. I took it home, then marvelled at it every day. Some things are just special, inanimate or not. I imagined the walks we'd take together along the beach (baby and I, obviously – not just Posh and I, okay? That would have been weird.), visits to the park, playdates with babies as yet unmet. I pictured mothers' coffee mornings, feeding the ducks, even taking baby to visit my old friends. In my mind's eye, I could see them fussing over this little novelty, impressed by my maturity, maybe somewhat jealous of my happiness and purpose.

A bit ambitious, probably. Considering that I hardly saw my friends once I'd left school, it was silly to think they'd have time for me and my baby-restricted lifestyle in their busy teenage social calendars. But I was a little stung by how ***easily*** they seemed to forget me, as if we hadn't been friends since primary school. You can't have everything, I suppose. I had other things on my mind and most of the time it didn't bother me terribly. I knew it was better that way. I was happy, but occasionally I caught a glimpse of my old life and it was strange that there was no room for me anymore.

Just how far we'd drifted apart became painfully apparent one January afternoon, when I decided to meet my friends at the school gates, just to say hi. I was nearly seven months pregnant then and way past the stage of trying to hide it. I couldn't have, even if I'd wanted to. I wasn't ashamed or embarrassed by my belly – by now it was just part of me, and I was often surprised when I spotted people staring. It always took a couple of seconds to realise what the hell they were gawking at. Ah yes, that would be me.

At the school gate, lots of people came up to say hello. Most were friendly, a few were not. It was nice to see my friends, but after the initial hugs hello and some tentative belly-rubbing, we stood around awkwardly, fresh out of anything to say to each other. We waited for a polite interval to elapse before we said our goodbyes and then bolted, all of us relieved. I realised I didn't want to hang around there any longer. I thought I'd be sad that it was so uncomfortable, but I actually wasn't. I think I needed to prove to myself that I was okay without them.

That I did, with a little help from a friend. At least, I thought she was a friend. Earlier on in my pregnancy, Cathy was the one who'd chirped so gleefully that I was lucky I didn't have to do PE anymore, since I had "an illegitimate reason". Yeah, I know, I should have smacked her. I was so dumb I thought we were laughing together. We were most assuredly not laughing together – not even close. She was having a go at me and I was too stupid to realise it. I shouldn't have been surprised by what happened next. But I was. Of course I was.

After saying goodbye to my other friends, I walked with her to the car, thinking I'd say hi to her mother. But as we approached the parking area, she started acting nervous, eyes darting back and forth – I thought she was scared of muggers or Nigerian drug dealers or something. Turns out she was just embarrassed to be seen with me.

I spotted her mother's car and was about to wave, when she squealed, "Quick, out the way before she sees you!" With that, she unceremoniously shoved me behind an oleander bush. Centre of gravity not being what it was, I stumbled and almost fell head first into the traffic. What a barrel of laughs.

I was more shocked than angry at first. Once I'd regained my balance (which took a while), I marched off in a huff and never spoke to her again. I just don't understand why some people have to be so damn nasty. And I couldn't believe that a person who'd once called herself my friend would rather have me chewing mouths full of poisonous plant while being driven over by a school bus, than have her mother realise I wasn't a virgin. I couldn't fathom what was so bad about me. I was still me, still the same, nice person I'd always been. I just had a really big stomach – visible proof that I'd once had sex. And what did that say about me? As far as I was concerned, all it said was that I'd once had sex. Juicy bit of info, to be sure, but how much did it really matter? It said nothing about how I'm kind to animals and beggars, how much I love my family, how determined I was to be a good mother and make my child proud. Nothing about the person in my head. I just don't get it.

I mean, how many other girls were bonking anything that moved, merrily and with reckless abandon, but just never got pregnant? Lots. Lots and lots of girls. And boys. The only difference was the lack of tangible evidence (if you didn't count the stray condom wrappers, often dishevelled clothing and ominous silences from bedrooms – all quite easy to detect if parents didn't have their heads so far up their butts). So parents could tell themselves this wasn't true, their children had been brought up better than to screw around and get pregnant. They could paddle around in the muddy waters of Denial, blissfully unaware that their offspring were banging one another like wanton rabbits, but that they had been lucky. So far. They hadn't yet spotted the Man-Eating Crocodile of Tragic Teenage Pregnancy floating silently, only its nostrils visible above the water, nor the Raging Hippo of Random Oozy Sexually Transmitted Diseases lurking there in the reeds.

It's all great fun until someone loses a leg.

***

Picture this. The place: Maintenance Office at local Magistrate's Court – a nightmare in dusty green-flecked lino and sound-proofed walls. The place existed in a time warp – a pristine example of early-eighties apartheid government institutional crapness.

The players: me, my giant belly (it was around the same time as the Oleander Bush Incident, so I was about seven months pregnant) and my grim-faced parents, David and his even more grim-faced mother, and lastly, an efficient, youngish, curly-haired social worker type.

We were here on a mission of grave consequence – to discuss David's financial contribution. Maintenance.

If I'd thought the daggers were bad the night we all met… well, I was wrong. There was so much sharp-edged weaponry flying across that room I'm surprised anybody was left standing.

Waiting for our appointment was torture. We all had to sit together on these horrific, wobbly, wooden benches flanking the walls of the passage. Side by side we sat, staring at the walls, at the scuffed, sticky tiles. Staring at anything rather than each other. Somehow, since David and I had broken up, relations between our families had gone from tactful, UN-style civility to full-on, Level One terror alert. I don't know how it happened, actually. I don't think David and I even spoke that day, except to say hello. It was all terribly awkward. I wished I could have been anywhere else at all – undergoing anaesthetic-free root canal treatment at the hands of a drunk, Parkinson's Disease-suffering dentist, for instance. Would have been a treat compared with this agony of bristling, embarrassed silence. The air crackled with dirty looks and bad vibes. As I watched, a fat fly buzzed slowly past us, straight into no-man's land, where it was struck with the force of five people's barely contained hostility. Death was instantaneous. The fly didn't suffer. He just stopped buzzing in mid-air and plopped onto the lino. All that was surprising was that he didn't burst into flame.

We were eventually called in, and after some uncomfortable musical chairs (You sit… No, really. I insist, you sit down – Somebody, somewhere, must know why there's always one bum more than chair), we got started. I was surprised when the maintenance lady spoke directly to me, and not to my parents.

"Right, so Tracy, what expenses do you expect to have? What do you need to buy for baby?" she asked. She'd done this before and was treating me no different to any of the other mothers she saw every day.

I was nervous. Didn't have a clue what to say. "Um… well, I already have most of the big things like a pram and cot and stuff…" I mumbled and stuttered, my cheeks burned – I've never been good at being the centre of attention. To be honest, I'd thought she would just give David a number and that would be it.

"Okay, well, what you should do is get a list together, and then we can work from there…" I nodded earnestly, trying not to look like the complete ignoramus that I was.

"Hang on…" David's mother had something to say. All eyes swivelled to her, David's face all thunder. He knew what was coming.

"How do we know it's even his child? We don't know that for sure", she said.

Oh my Gawd! Bloody gobsmacked, I was. My flabbers were utterly gasted. Was this woman serious? Why had she never brought this up before? Did she really think I'd been sleeping around? Or was she just trying to find a way out of the money issue?

David snorted in disgust and shook his head. He mumbled something about "being ridiculous". They'd been through this before, I was sure.

My father may have jumped up and said something like "Now see here lady…"

I just sat there, my mouth hanging open, my cheeks threatening to spontaneously combust. I wanted to cry. I wanted to smack her. But no, I just sat. Maintenance Lady quickly tried to bring some calm and rationality to the situation, to defuse the coming apocalypse before things got too heated and she missed her tea break. I swear, I saw her look at the clock.

"Now, I really don't think that's an issue. I mean, we're talking about a fourteen-year-old girl here," she said in a reasonable tone of voice. I could have kissed her – I forgave the indiscreet clockwatching, she was, of course, legally entitled to her tea break and I wouldn't dream of keeping her from it. Suddenly she was my new best friend. She turned to me.

"Tracy, is it David's child? Are you sure about that?" I guess she had to ask.

"Yes, I'm sure. Of course I'm sure."

She seemed to accept that and no more was said about it. David's mother wasn't happy. She didn't believe me – okay, not entirely accurate. She didn't ***want*** to believe me, but yes, she knew. Just like David knew, and had tried to convince her. That meant something to me. He didn't have to speak up against his mother that day. He could have kept quiet and forced me into a paternity test and more complications. But he didn't. I should remember that more often. It should count for something.

The rest of the meeting passed by in a blur. I went home and made my list of expenses (lists being my thing, as you know), but we never handed it in and ended up not claiming maintenance from David at all.

***

Well, there you have it. My pregnancy in a nutshell. Physically, it was just an ordinary pregnancy like any other. Emotionally, it was more complicated. But I got through it. Once out of school, I enjoyed being pregnant. I loved my belly. I loved feeling my baby move. I loved learning about pregnancy, birth and parenthood. I threw myself into it, I embraced it all, and I think I did a good job.

My studying was going well and as a family we were finding our equilibrium, a new way of being with each other. And I was finding out who I really was. It was a special time for me, and I'll always be grateful for it. Of course, I had moments of doubt, but every mother does. Maybe my doubts were more justifiable, maybe more amplified, given my youth, but I never once said I'd changed my mind. As afraid as I was, I knew I was doing the right thing. Although I worried and obsessed that I'd be a terrible mother, somewhere deep down I knew we'd be fine. That little voice that had first spoken to me on the day I found out I was pregnant was positively chatty now – it felt like the voice of my child, coming from a different time and place. A time and place of ***before*** – the place he'd been waiting for me, until I was ready for him.

The voice reassured me, comforted me, encouraged me to be brave. I so wanted to meet him. But first, my biggest challenge. The birth. Of course, I was convinced I'd never be able to do it. I've since learnt that everybody feels that way. Knowing that wouldn't have helped at all, though. I was scared shitless (although that's not entirely correct, given the whole enema debacle. Had I been truly scared shitless, I may have been spared that humiliation.)

Chapter Five

1994: In which she gets high and falls down a lot (in unrelated events)

Steven Engelbrecht made his grand entrance at 16h20 on 11 April 1994, exactly on his due date, and while I was already at the hospital having a routine check up. Most considerate of him. He's been big on punctuality, even from birth. That's my boy.

April 11 was Baby Day, but nobody really expected him to arrive on time. First babies don't usually, after all. Or so I was told. By the same strange people who told me, alternately, that I was either "carrying high" or "carrying low" or "carrying in front" or "carrying behind". Whatever. I never did get the whole "carrying" thing. It's not like he was a Checkers packet or French loaf or something. Still, they sounded so ***knowledgeable***, so ***convinced*** of their arguments, it was easy to believe they knew more than you, particularly when they employed that specially patented patronising-yet-soothing tone no-one dared oppose.

These people (that would be nosy women) are the Old Wives referred to in the saying. They're called Old Wives because most of them are – having been married for roughly a thousand years and having had their children back in the day when penicillin was big news. They can actually be a good source of information at times, but you have to listen with your Bullshit Filter turned all the way up. They have loads of experience, but many of them also seem to have an innate need to frighten the pants off anyone standing still long enough to listen to their Cousin Freda's horrific gauze-left-in-the-uterus Caesarean story. I'd encountered a few of these biddies, and had been shocked to find that several antenatal nurses were actually secret members of the Old Wives Club. Never mind all that modern hooey about breast is best, they'd quietly tell their confused patients. That's just what the doctors want us to say. Everyone knows what newborn babies really need is supplemental bottle feeding with sugar water, and bring on the honey-covered dummies, too.

I had a regular weekly check-up scheduled for that day, so off we went at nine in the morning. I left my maths revision open on my desk, fully expecting to get back to it by about lunchtime. As it turned out, it would stay open on the trinomial factorisation page for the next four weeks.

Monday was Antenatal Clinic day at the hospital. Preggie fairies of all shapes, sizes and ages gathered to be poked and prodded by bossy nurses and busy doctors. So many different women, all doing and feeling exactly the same things. Same aching backs, same swollen feet, same gaseous digestive issues. Watching them all fascinated me. I was amazed that I was one of them, with my very own aches and escalating paranoia.

The lady with the swollen feet really scared me. She could barely walk and she couldn't wear shoes. Her pork sausagey ankles looked like they would burst like water balloons if poked. Not that you'd want to; you'd probably pay good money to avoid poking those squidgy ankles. She didn't have long to wait. As soon as the nurses got a look at those tremendous feet, she was bustled into the doctor's office and then, amid great fanfare and official-form-filling-in, to the labour ward. Other women nodded to each other knowingly and the whisper rippled through the waiting room like a juicy office rumour – pre-eclampsia. A shudder went down every spine. We all imagined ourselves being wheeled off to an emergency Caesar at thirty-four weeks; frantic phone calls to husbands (or not, if you were me); things going wrong.

The nurse did all the usual things before I saw the doctor. She checked my blood pressure (a bit low, but it usually was); my cunningly pre-packaged urine sample (no trace of anything dodge); my haemoglobin (ze aitch-bee, remember? Also low – got the "you should be eating liver" lecture); weighed me (62 kilograms at nine months pregnant – oh, to be fifteen years old again!), and assured me that the funny, twangy cramps I'd been feeling all weekend were probably just Braxton Hicks contractions. I was the picture of fat pregnant health and everything was going according to plan. Thus far.

"Is everything alright?" was the theme for every doctor's visit. And, so far, everything had been fine. My baby was growing wonderfully, all milestones were being reached and all measurements correct. Against all odds, it seemed I would deliver a strong, healthy baby – a strapping young lad.

I hadn't found out the baby's sex, but I had a strong "boy feeling". My doctor was lovely – a big, kindly teddy-bear of a man who explained things so nicely and never once made me want to kick him in the nuts. That was a big deal for me. I was oversensitive about everything and the smallest perceived skew look or funny comment would set me off. But he never did anything to make me uncomfortable. I was looking forward to having him at the birth. He had a very calming effect on me, and I felt I'd do all right with him.

And then. Just as I was beginning to feel comfortable and mildly confident, do you know what the bugger did? Do you know? He got himself transferred to Namibia, that's what he did. The horrible, horrible man went away without telling me, so I was left in the lurch on my due date, not knowing who would deliver my baby.

I didn't take this news well. I was unsettled and worried and beginning to have a terribly dark suspicion about that twelve-year-old boy dressed up as a doctor who'd just picked up my file. No... please no.... don't tell me you're my new doctor...

Worry turned to borderline hysteria as he called my name. Of course. Of course he's the doctor. How could I have thought any different? I couldn't believe it. He was yummy, but so very, very young. He looked more like a teenager than I did. Surely this wasn't allowed? Did they really let unqualified children wander around here without supervision? Where's the real doctor? That's what I'd like to know. Where's the fricking camera? I know Leon Schuster must be here somewhere, the bastard. I cringed as I followed him into the office, the thought of explaining my Situation to this kid whom I might otherwise have attempted to flirt with giving me cramps.

Dr Boy Wonder's friendly, reassuring smile and quite adorable bedside manner didn't help one bit. My confidence had been seriously rattled and I was on the verge of tears. Again. What a surprise.

He read my file and noted my latest blood pressure reading and other vital statistics.

"Hmmm… everything here looks good. The sister tells me you've been having cramps this weekend?" he asked. Ever so professional, but I was still waiting for the punchline.

"I tell you what, let's have a look. If the pains weren't regular, it's probably just Braxton Hicks." He paused tactfully, in case I didn't know what Braxton Hicks were. Of course I knew. Snotty know-it-all kid. "But let's make sure, shall we? Hop up onto the bed and we'll check you out." Another reassuring smile, which also made no difference.

Hmph. Check me out indeed. The nerve. So, not only was this little boy going to sit there and be all condescending, now he wanted to go prospecting too? Wonderful. I wondered briefly whether he was some kind of perv from the paediatric psych ward in a stolen white coat. I wasn't convinced by his official name badge or fancy stethoscope. He was a pretend doctor, a Doogie Howser, a George Clooney – entertaining and easy on the eye, but you wouldn't let him anywhere near a real patient.

I stripped and got up onto the bed. Of course I did. For all my stroppy bravado, I was still a sucker for authority, real or fraudulent. Wuss.

I'd thought I was over the embarrassment of gynaecological examinations. I'd been wrong. I didn't mind Teddy Bear Doctor. He was ***old.*** He knew what he was doing. This guy, on the other hand, was a whole new ball game. I was very aware of how young and handsome he was, and that he was poking around in places where young and handsome males of the species do not as a rule poke, except under completely different circumstances.

I lay there with my legs up, as you do, and tried to think of something to say. My meagre store of small talk had been erased from my brain, unfortunately, so I lay there in silence, waiting for him to finish. He seemed to be taking awfully long.

Then he said "IImmm." Just likc that. Hmmm. What the hell did that mean?

He fiddled and faffed a bit more, then asked, "These pains you were feeling, how strong were they? Are you still getting them?" Very calm, very doctor-like, but I was freaking out. Okay, so now I'm worried.

"No, they stopped on Sunday. I haven't had anymore. They just felt funny, almost like period pains, but not really. Why?" I asked in a quivery, soggy sort of voice. Tell me what the fuck is going on here please? But I didn't say that.

"Hmmm," he said again, as he took another look. Not very helpful, I must say. Then he straightened up, snapped off those rubber gloves and grinned at me.

"Are you quite sure you're not feeling any contractions right now? Because you're five centimetres dilated, and I think it's time to admit you."

Oh, holy God. ***What? This*** was definitely not in the plan. How could I be five centimetres dilated, half-way there, without having felt anything? What happened to timing contractions, waters breaking dramatically in the street, frantic midnight drives to the hospital? What happened to all the stuff the book said about first labours taking a long time? And most of all how could it possibly be time ***now***? Just like that, no big deal, no time to prepare or get used to the idea. No hanging around for hours trying to decide if it's time to go to the hospital or not. No time for reality to sink in slowly. Just sommer bung me in a hospital gown and stick me in a bed. Just like that. Yes, I know – I'd had nine months to get used to the idea, But still, this seemed unfair. I felt ambushed. I felt like he'd sprung this on me just to be mean.

And he looked so damn cheerful. Clearly, he thought this was wonderful.

"Come on, then, get dressed. Is your mom here with you? Let's go tell her the good news," he said. Grinning damn idiot. I was frozen to the spot and couldn't seem to feel my legs.

Eventually I managed to pull myself together, and we walked back into the waiting room. He took me over to the reception desk and got my file in order for the admitting procedure. My mom looked worried as she watched us pass – this was a new development, the doctor didn't usually come out with me.

I went over to Mom and whispered, “He says it’s time. He says I have to be admitted now.” All shaky-voiced again.

“What?! NOW?!” she squealed, trying to be quiet, but with the whole room on high-alert, they heard every word.

“Yes, that’s what he says, Ma. He says I’m five centimetres dilated. It’s time.”

And so it was.

Lots of excitement and activity followed. We filled in all the forms at Admissions, where another very young desk clerk asked, “Reason for admittance?” He was serious, too. The enormous tummy and hefty hospital bag I was lugging were perhaps not obvious enough clues for him.

“Um… it would seem I’m in labour”, I replied. Duh. He printed what seemed like ten thousand sheets of sticky labels with my name and file number and other details on. What the hell they were all for was anyone’s guess. Clearly, printing labels was his job and he was enthusiastically committed to doing it. I might also mention that it was somewhere at this juncture that, under “religion”, someone checked “Roman Catholic” on my file. The military hospital was clearly keen on religion and you had to pick something. I’d seen through the whole church racket by then and couldn’t call myself Catholic, even though my father was a Catholic. Had I checked the box myself, I probably would have picked “Other”. So perhaps I can blame the dumb young office clerk for the horrors that were to come.

In the labour ward, I unpacked my bag and then subjected myself to another battery of physical checks. Then I sat. For at least two hours I sat around, extremely bored and feeling like an impostor. I heard other women in the throes of labour, some of them going about it quite loudly. I saw large, sweaty-haired women lurching along the passages, supported by panic-stricken husbands glancing around for the nearest exit. Rats in a trap, they were. I saw them look at me, trying to figure me out. It didn't look like I was in labour, so just what was I doing here, then? I felt sheepish, as if I was intruding where I didn't belong. And still, I didn't feel any contractions.

I had more internal exams, and matters were apparently progressing. Still – nothing.

Eventually, around noon, it was decided that they'd have to break my waters. Which they did. With an enormous crochet hook – I still see its evil pointy head in my dreams sometimes.

Once the waters were broken, I began to feel some pain. The labour was going well, but I was nervous and tense. The tenser I got, the worse the pain got, which prompted the nurse to ask whether I wanted to try some gas for pain relief.

"No! No, I don't want it! I don't need it!" I insisted, weakly.

"Now, don't try and be brave, my girl. There's nothing wrong with a little gas, you don't have to feel guilty about it, you know," she said.

Oh, but I did. Good mothers (which I was determined to be) did not accept pain relief during labour. Good mothers focused on their baby's face and imagining him making his way out of the birth canal (birth canal – what a truly heinous phrase. As if you're likely to find a couple of crooning gondoliers floating about in there) to meet you and the world. Good mothers don't need that shit. Good mothers are strong.

Guilt gland – activate. The Guilt gland is standard onboard equipment for any mother. They trigger as soon as you know there's a baby inside you. And they never shut down again after that, not until you die. I suspect they keep working even after you die (like the way the hair on corpses sometimes keeps growing after death. Eeeuw!), leaching free-range guilt into the soil, to be taken up by the plants that we end up eating. Like oestrogen in the water. Only not.

The guilt gland can malfunction sometimes – it can be overactive or underactive (much like the thyroid) – but you can't take a pill to fix it. Well, you could. But they're mostly illegal. However, my guilt gland was brand new and still getting warmed up. Which explains why I gave in to the idea of sniffing the happy gas on offer.

I hated myself, but oh – did I love that gas. It made me high immediately – and while it didn't take the pain away, it relaxed my body so completely that between contractions I lapsed into near unconsciousness. I wasn't fighting the pain anymore. I was going with it. The contractions became more intense, I shouted at my mother louder and more often as soon as she stopped rubbing my back – and the day wore on.

In the midst of all this, some crazy person brought me lunch – roast lamb, potatoes and veg. I was impressed – not bad grub for a government facility, I thought. Unfortunately, the sight of it still made me want to puke. I couldn't bear the thought of eating, so the plate just sat there the whole way through my labour, slowly and greasily congealing in the corner. How gross. Stupid, stupid me. If I'd known of the microwaved abominations that were in store, I would have chowed down, drug-induced nausea or not.

Then, suddenly, I had to push. Don't ask me how I knew – I'd never believed women when they said you just know what to do. I'd always thought I'd be the only person to whom this did not apply. But what do you know? It turns out I was a real live Natural Woman who could do these things. Somewhere underneath the brain fog and abject terror, I was quite proud of myself.

It's amazing what those four little words can do. Yell (or whisper) "I need to push" in a labour ward and see everybody spring into action. Like a race car I was wheeled into the delivery ward just before four in the afternoon. I was exhausted. Giving birth is the only way on earth you ever get as tired as that. I struggled to get the pushing right – it was one step forward, two steps back.

I remember repeatedly crying to the midwife and nurses, "I'm sorry, I'm sorry!"

Even in that state, I was convinced that I was doing it all wrong, probably wasting their time, annoying them and keeping them from their hot dinners. The guilt gland was in overdrive now, and my self-consciousness was getting in the way of the birth process. I was thinking too much, instead of doing.

Then somebody called, "One last push, Tracy! One last push, we're nearly there!"

And I did it, just when I thought I could do no more. One last push.

And there he was. My baby. I laughed and I cried. He was quiet.

"It's a boy! You've got a little boy, Tracy!" the midwife called as she wrapped him in a blanket and handed him to me.

"A boy… my boy…" I held him on my chest, my arms so wobbly I was scared I'd drop him. I looked at him so hard, wanting to sear his image into my brain forever, in case it wasn't real and somebody came and took him away. But they couldn't, could they? Nobody could take him away. He was mine. And I was glad.

"What's his name?" asked the nurse. I thought I'd say Ethan. That was the name I'd chosen, after all. But that's not what I said.

"Steven. His name is Steven," I replied, without the slightest clue where that had come from. Steven. Of course, Steven. He wasn't Ethan at all. He was Steven – you could tell that just by looking at him.

Steven lay on my chest, quiet, not crying, his big eyes open and absorbing everything around him. Even then, he was so aware. Oh, I was overcome by how lucky I was. Surely nobody else in the world had ever felt this amazing. The pain was forgotten, vanished in an instant (another thing I hadn't believed possible), and what was left was invincibility and joy. In those moments, I knew what it was all about. I knew what it had all been for. I knew that it had all been worth it.

Is there something else out there for me? Now I knew, and here it was.

When they took him to be cleaned up, I cried, half thinking I'd never get him back. But that's just silly, I guess.

Then came the stitching up of the episiotomy cut, which took longer than the delivery and wasn't half as much fun. I kept asking the midwife whether she was finished, and she kept laughing and saying she'd only just started. My toes still curl at the mere thought of those damn stirrups.

The rest of the afternoon passed in a blur. I was still high and woozy from the gas, and it had knocked me out completely. They wheeled me back to the Recovery Ward and I slept all the way, waking only briefly to scream when they mashed my fingers between the wheely-bed and the door as they were moving me into the ward.

While I was being stitched up and resting, the nurse had found my mother and asked whether she wanted to hold Steven. And she did. Mom stood alone with him in a tiny room, the two of them together, getting to know each other. That's when my mother realised everything would be okay. She understood that she loved him; she really did, even though she had been worried that she wouldn't. She realised he was part of our family, he ***belonged.*** With us. Not an outsider, not a burden, not a constant reminder of pain or disappointment. Just a special little person with a place in our home. Our boy.

I always get a lump in my throat when Mom talks about the time she spent with Steven on his first day in the world. It sounds so special, so private.

I had so much to be grateful for that day.

But the first night was truly awful. I'd never felt worse in my life. The pain, the tiredness, the absolute yuckiness of all these unfamiliar bodily functions. I came around at about nine, and I heard a TV in the background somewhere. Some big debate was going on between Nelson Mandela and FW De Klerk. Frankly, at that point I couldn't have cared less. All I wanted was to be clean, warm and not so damn ***oozy.*** And to sleep, of course. I wanted to go home.

When I needed the loo, I was too exhausted to get out of bed and got all panicked. I tried to ring for the nurse but couldn't remember which button to press. I pressed them all and nothing happened, except for my bed jerking up and down a few times, causing further panic and adding seasickness to the mix. Either the buttons were out of order, or the nurses were simply ignoring me. I looked at a little white buzzer marked "Chaplain" and reflected on the horribleness, yet comforting practicality of that idea. Eventually, a nurse came around and helped me to the loo. She helped me get cleaned up and changed, and twice caught me as I fainted. Something to do with blood loss and anaemia – damn, I wished I'd eaten more liver.

The nurses fed Steven that night. Earlier, they'd given me instructions about collecting formula and bottles and timing of feeds, but I admit I didn't catch any of it. I was just so tired, so very out of it – in no state to look after Steven. I was in no state to look after myself, either. I was a wreck, crying (of course), leaking and aching all over the place. Perhaps it was a reaction to the gas, but my age probably also had something to do with how messed up I was.

It was a good thing that Steven was kept in the nursery that night, because he wasn't keeping any of his feeds down. They told me this the next morning, when I'd eventually woken up and they brought him to me. Obviously I panicked.

"Why? What's wrong? Is he sick?" I asked, terrified.

No, no, they assured me. They'd just change the formula and he'd be fine.

But he wasn't fine. He didn't keep any feeds down at all over the next day and a half, and eventually they moved him to Paediatric ICU and put him on a drip. You can imagine what that did to my fragile nerves. The sight of my helpless baby with a nasty-looking drip attached to his little shaved head just broke my heart. I felt completely powerless. I couldn't do anything to help him and it was probably somehow my fault that he was sick, too. The nurses and doctors didn't do much to make me feel better. They seemed vague and nonchalant about the whole thing. They certainly didn't keep me informed about what they were doing, or why they were doing it. Perhaps they thought I wouldn't understand their fancy medical terms, or maybe they thought I didn't care. It's my fault too, though. I just accepted things and was too intimidated to ask questions. Another symptom of the Grown-Ups Know Best disease, which had plagued me all my life. I'm cured these days, of course, but only because I'm a grown-up myself and realise I don't know shit.

Every day I walked (staggered) from my ward to the ICU where Steven lay, to feed him and be with him. I'd sit next to his bassinette in the stifling heat of the ICU, hold his hand and sing funny little cartoon theme songs to him. I told him about his home, the bedroom that was waiting for him, and his family who loved him. I told him I needed him to get better, and if he only would, I promised to never let him down. I promised him the world, then cried because I thought I might not be able to deliver on my promises.

Nobody could tell me what was wrong with him. Whatever it was, it couldn't have been too bad. Compared with the other poor tiny babies in the ICU – premature and sickly – he looked solid and healthy. He was awake most of the time, and the nurses had moved his bassinette to the big window, so that he could look out and see the sky and the trees. I know it was way too soon for him to focus, but I'd swear he was aware. He was a quiet, calm baby who didn't cry much. He just lay there watching with his big, blue eyes and you just knew he was taking it all in.

At least three times a day I trudged along the corridors to the ICU in my dressing gown and gigantic panda slippers. And at least three times a day I fainted while doing so. I lost count of the number of times I had to be rescued and taken back to my bed in a wheelchair. Most embarrassing. Especially the time I passed out directly underneath the window to the nurses' station and lay on the floor for ages before anybody noticed.

Eventually they figured out that I'd lost too much blood and a transfusion was scheduled. Which meant I had to stay in hospital another day. Bugger. But rather that than constant swooning.

Transfusion was a nightmare. Two bags of saline and some crazy amount of blood. Of course, this being me, the drip got blocked and stopped running. When the nurse removed the drip, the blockage was released and a giant fountain of blood shot up out of my arm and hit the ceiling. I kid you not.

And the food. Oh my God. Never have I seen such lumpy porridge, such desiccated, wrinkly gem squash, such grey boerewors. And don't get me started on the eggs. Or the unidentifiable white, gelatinous mass presented as pudding. It was criminal. I couldn't bring myself to eat much and I lived on oranges and chocolates from visitors.

The food was gross, the blood and guts were awful, but these weren't the worst of my hospital horrors. The very worst misery came in the form of a tiny, wrinkly nun with a giant score to settle.

Spiritual counsel must have been part of the warm, fuzzy government hospital service; hence the religion question on the admission forms. However, the delegate sent to counsel me was as spiritual as a Jiffy bag full of piranhas.

Sister Maria Enchilada scuttled into my room one morning after breakfast and I put on my Talking To Official Grown-Ups Face. She was very, very old. Very short. So very, very Catholic. But I wasn't scared. Nuns are supposed to be wonderful, special, enlightened people, right? Full of God's love and all that.

Well, now. I'd been misinformed. She didn't get the memo re God's love. She was still working on the eternal damnation specs. And why not? Stick with what you know, and she was good at it.

"So, are you going to marry this man?" she asked haughtily. She'd been checking out my file and had noticed a big blank space where "spouse" should have been. I admit, I laughed. God, I laughed at a nun! There must be a particular punishment regimen for that. Ten Hail Mary's just ain't gonna cut it.

"No, of course I'm not going to marry him. That would be a very unwise decision." I tried to look serious, but she was not amused.

The second time Sister Maria Enchilada came around, she was steaming with anger.

"You're only fifteen years old!" she yelled. "I thought you were about twenty! How can you even show your face here? You're a disgusting example to your younger sister! The ***shame*** you're subjecting your family to! You're going to hell, my girl…"

And on, and on. She yelled at me in her squeaky, old-lady voice until I thought her wrinkly, walnut head was going to completely unscrew and fly across the room. Where I would catch it and stomp on it a bit, until I felt better.

What can you say to that? You can't argue with a nun. So I bit my tongue and waited for her to disappear.

The third time she visited, I spotted her beforehand and hid in the toilet until she went away.

I went home five days later, but Steven had to stay. Going home without him was the hardest thing I'd ever done. But they wanted to make sure he was okay. They were waiting until he'd gained back a little weight, which he did that weekend. They called me on Sunday to say I could fetch him.

I dressed him in his special homecoming suit, which was miles too big. I even managed to put his nappy on straight, and he weed on me only a little. I was doing well. I said goodbye to the nurses, wrapped him in his little elephant blanket and very, very carefully carried him out to the car.

I was taking my boy home. He was really here now. He was really mine. No going back. Wow.

Chapter Six

1994: In which she figures out which way is up, eventually

Bringing Steven home from the hospital was surreal. I walked outside into the lemony April sunlight and the whole world seemed completely different. It was a different planet, as if I'd woken from a coma after thirty years to find that men had walked on the moon. Or something. The world in my head had changed so dramatically, so permanently, I was sure I'd see the change outside, too. After what I'd just done, how could anything in the world still be the same?

We were all on cloud nine and, in our excitement over-ambitious, which led to a grave error in judgment. Why not go straight from the hospital to visit Gran and my great aunts and uncles? What a lovely idea, we thought. Everyone wanted to see Steven, and I wanted to show him off. Big mistake. Huge.

There is a reason why the books say you should limit visitors in the first few days, and it's not only because you'll be a red-eyed zombie with baby puke for hair gel. Of course you will be. Or because you need the time to bond in private, although you need that, too. No – it's actually so that you don't scare friends and relatives by revealing what an absolutely bungling disaster of a useless, reject mother you truly are. The books should quit beating about the bush and say this directly. It could save many an over-confident new mother the embarrassment of being dragged off to the Child Welfare offices by concerned mothers-in-law who have witnessed the first solo, nurse-free attempts at breastfeeding. Nobody likes to look stupid. But believe me, you are guaranteed to look monumentally stupid. So best you do it in the privacy of your own home, without any witnesses besides those directly involved and as inept as you are. Or ones you can send to sleep with the fishes without arousing too much suspicion.

I didn't know this then, obviously, so off we went to visit the relatives. What can I say? It seemed like a good idea at the time. Of course, so did the second George Bush, and we all know how that turned out.

I've never been on a more terrifying drive than that day, not even the time an angry policeman ex-boyfriend drove me home ten minutes after me dumping him. As always, my mother drove perfectly, but now we seemed to be surrounded by danger on every side – crazy, reckless road hogs, stray cows, drunk pedestrians, crater-sized potholes. Perils I'd never noticed before. They seemed to have come out especially for the occasion, hell-bent on our annihilation. I held my bundle of breakable porcelain in my arms and sat with my eyes screwed shut all the way there, bracing myself for the moment of impact. I was surprised when it didn't happen and we arrived in one piece.

While the family oohed and aahed, Steven was a little angel and didn't fuss at all, even when passed from one cooing old lady to the next – another big Miriam Stoppard no-no. I was ordered to sit down and relax. (Ha ha! Tell that to a new mother on her first day home with baby and see where it gets you.) Meanwhile, various interchangeable aunties mollycoddled and reminisced on days gone by, when you stayed in bed for two weeks after giving birth. The word Confinement was mentioned a lot. Sounded like scarlet fever to me, but I was too polite to say so. (***Oh Marmee, it's Beth; she's caught the consumption…*** Why do the words quinine and ipecac spring to mind? What the hell is quinine anyway? Not sure I care to know about the ipecac. Actually, I don't think it was Beth. I think it was Amy. Jo was the one who cut all her hair off, I do remember that. It's been a while. I may even be confusing ***Little Women*** with ***Anne of Green Gables.*** God, I loved Anne. So much cooler than that wench Pollyanna. And Gilbert… wow! Unfortunate name, but yummie boy, all the same.)

I soon realised the visit had been a bad idea. It was fraught with tension. I was touchy and took every offer of help as a condemnation of my as yet non-existent mothering skills. Hey, it's not paranoia if they're really after you, right? Oh, but I was wrong about that. So wrong. Nobody was after me then, and they still aren't (except a select few – ***you know who you are***). It's taken me years to get this. And I still find it hard to remember.

Do you know how much time I've wasted obsessing over what people thought of me, staggering under the weight of the giant chip on my shoulder – so tightly wound, always on my best behaviour, because you never know who might be watching and making notes in the Bumper Compendium of Bad Mothers. I'm sure living on cigarettes, vodka and Big Macs for thirteen years would have been a healthier option than spending all that time dissecting every look, every inflection in every word, even those of perfect strangers – people I'd never see again. Scrutinising every move from every angle until pretty soon you forget what you're looking for, or looking at. I should have a bleeding stomach ulcer by now.

I held it together until it was time to feed and change him. Bear in mind this was my first time outside the hospital. And I'd be staging the performance in front of half a dozen extremely helpful elderly relatives whom I didn't know all that well. Mom could tell my nerves were shot, so she rescued me from my embarrassing, emotionally-scarring nappy fumbling. She bustled in and took over, straightening the pitiful nappy and wiping the rogue Fissan Paste off the upholstery. That done, she began supervising bottle-making, telling me how to measure out the milk powder correctly (level spoonfuls, Tracy – don't forget!). Again, big mistake.

Formula: take one anal-retentive, perfectionist Good Girl, add enough rampaging hormones to float a small barge, nine months' worth of corrosive guilt and fear, performance anxiety too large for any little blue pill to overcome and the absolute knowledge that your child will soon die of starvation, because the lumps in the formula just won't go away. Into this heady mix, throw an audience of Old Wives and a jittery mother trying her level best to make it all better by doing it herself. What do you get? Nuclear meltdown, that's what. I was spitting mad with everybody. I felt the beginnings of a tantrum coming on (I recognise the signs when my throat clenches up and my temples throb). I was close to shouting at everybody to bugger off and leave me and my child alone, interfering, patronising old crones, the lot of them. I should have done it, too. It would have been terribly rude, but it would have made me feel better for a minute. As it was, the most I could manage was – gasp – shooting a ***very*** withering glare in their direction, accompanied by bonus passive-aggressive sigh.

Strained and jumpy herself – she could smell an outburst at a hundred metres – Mom caught my ostentatious sigh (as she always does), and asked what was wrong.

"Nothing!" I snapped, unconvincingly. "I'm fine! There's nothing wrong!" ***Woof***. Communication had never been my thing, I admit. It was always, Nothing, or Fine, neither response ever being true. They just served to stand in for the things I couldn't say. Like blank Scrabble tiles. They can mean anything you want them to. Oh man, I've done it now. I should never have admitted that. If you ask me again, I'll blankly deny it. Deny, deny, deny. It's the Area 51 of emotional dysfunction; we just don't go there. But this is one admission I know will come back to bite me in the ass before long.

While Mom changed and fed Steven, I hovered like a waitress on her first day. He didn't seem particularly interested in the feeding part of the process. This was an ominous sign, one I should have paid attention to.

All the way through, I found myself doing a fabulous Obnoxious Moody Teenager impression. Panic and misery set in as I saw myself relinquishing responsibility for my child. This wasn't how it was supposed to go. I was supposed to be doing all this stuff, warming hearts with my natural flair for motherhood. Had we been home, of course, this would all have been different. Instead of reacting defensively to my mother's help, I would have welcomed it, I imagine. But there, out of my depth and surrounded by what I imagined to be a hostile audience, I thought I'd lost him. Given him up. So soon, without even having tried properly. I felt like an utter failure. And since I was damned if I were going to cry in front of everybody, it came across as sulking.

Alarm bells must have been ringing in everybody's heads: "Look at that. It had to happen. Her mother's doing everything. She can't be bothered to look after her child herself. And that attitude…"

Worst-case scenario – sad but inevitable – Irresponsible Teenage Mother Lets Child Down, And Long-Suffering Granny Takes Charge. My dear mother was only trying to help, to take the pressure, the scrutiny, off me, and somewhere under the turmoil of my freak-out I knew that.

Still, I badly wanted to wrest Steven away from her, to screech: "Let me see to my own child, goddammit! Do I look like an idiot?" Or, "If one more person touches that baby, I'm going to fucking chop their hands off!"

I held it together and didn't swear at any old ladies, but it was a close thing. My bitchy sighs and eye-rolling were noted by all and the rest of the visit was tense and awful. All the fun had gone out of it. I'd hurt my mother's feelings. She thought I didn't appreciate her help, and her own instinctive reaction kicked in – the one that goes, "Fine! I'll never help you again! I'll just keep away from you, that's obviously what you want!"

I felt clueless, selfish and lazy. And on top of that, I'd hardly had any time with Steven at all. I needed to take him home, to lie with him on my bed, to talk to him, to hold him, learn about him and love him. At our own pace and in our own place. Home. Yet, there we sat. Drinking weak tea out of flowery porcelain cups, while struggling to keep our heads in line with those damn antimacassars. (That is what they're called, right? Those crocheted jobs made fashionable in the 1950s and placed over the backs of chairs and couches to absorb the Brilliantine off the heads of the menfolk? Question: What the heck is a macassar and why do we have to be anti them? What has the poor macassar ever done to us? Where are the promacassars?)

I watched the smug, hateful grandfather clock all afternoon. Every time I looked, it seemed to have stopped ticking. It was always just five minutes after the last time I'd checked. Tick… tick… tick…

An eternity passed before the clock struck the magical hour of five o'clock, when all good visitors must go, when they begin to indicate their intention by fidgeting and making tentative, polite noises of, We Should Think About Making A Move… I barely restrained myself from whooping with relief, racing around to gather up Steven's paraphernalia. I was half-way down the garden path, baby and bag in tow, while Mom was still graciously refusing one last cup of tea and fending off foil-wrapped slices of fruitcake and onion bread proffered on such occasions.

Just take the fricking fruitcake, for God's sake! (Why always fruitcake, by the way?) Graciously accept the baked goods and do a runner before they remember the tea again! Takeaway confectionery is a bonus in any household. And stale confectionary could be used as building material or blunt-force trauma murder weapon, should the need arise.

After what seemed like weeks, we were home. Ever so carefully, I carried my boy down the front steps and into the house. It was a special moment. Finally, all the drama and pain seemed to be at an end. We were together at last, all of us, and it was right. I cried. Yet again.

But as wonderful as it was to be home, the first night was hell. Much production was made of bath time, the fiendish occult horror that is night feeds still waiting in the wings.

"Do you really think we should bath him now?" asked my mother, timidly. I was puzzled by the question.

Yes yes, of course! I've got all these lovely bath-time gadgets and equipment and smellies… of course we bath him. Why ever not? That's what good mothers do, isn't it? Bath their babies? Right? Am I missing something? I must have missed something. Dammit. Is there some rule I'm not aware of?

Obviously I didn't say any of this to her. The mere fact that she'd asked the question in that nervous I-don't-think-it's-a-good-idea-but-don't-dare-suggest-it tone indicated that she had something on her mind. Hmm… try as I might, I couldn't figure it out, so I was forced to reveal my ignorance. I hate that.

"Um, you don't think we should bath him, Ma? Why not?" I asked, equally timidly.

And there it was. The defining moment. The beginning of our astounding, record-breaking feats of Walking on Eggshells. We did it then, we do it now. We're really good at it. Call it tact or diplomacy, call it beating about the bush or choosing our words carefully to minimise damage, we're the champions. We have, on occasion, slipped up and accidentally let rip with what we really think and feel, but not often. I recall a particularly nasty fight during which I lost it and threw a soggy, disposable nappy across the room, narrowly missing my dear mother's head. Good times…

"Um … you know, it's quite late already. Don't you think it's a bit cold to bath him now?" Ma cringed as she said it. She must have had premonitions of projectile nappies.

Oh dear. I had missed something. Six hours into this motherhood lark and I'm already about to give my child hypothermia. Nice.

I bristled. (Yeah, that's such a good word. Describes the sensation perfectly: the little hairs on my arms rising, leg and jaw muscles tensing as irritation seethed within.) I bristled mostly because she was right and I was stupid – but also because of those three words she uses every time she tries to sound casual and nonchalant. ***Don't you think…?*** That little phrase ***so*** pisses me off, for no rational reason at all. I seems to say, "Why the hell didn't ***you*** think of this?"

Ah – but then, oh joy and hallelujah – I was saved. I remembered the chapter on bath time in one of my many second-hand baby books. I think it was the one whose pages are populated entirely by women with long, straight hair parted down the middle, or else permed beyond recognition, wearing brown polyester sundresses and false eyelashes. The words "Your husband" are used a lot in that one. Lots of soft-focus shots of mother holding baby, and zero pictures of breastfeeding. Which is crazy, because that's what you really need, right? Actual photographs of actual women breastfeeding actual babies, so that you can see exactly what you're supposed to do. When you come right down to it, what does a properly latched baby ***look*** like, dammit? We need to know these things. Apparently, in 1975, vague descriptions were good enough. Probably explains why an entire generation of children was bottle fed. You don't need to use the word "nipple" to explain bottle feeding, much less flash any real ones. Oh, the horror!

According to the Sacred Illustrated Text of Smug Seventies Motherhood, it is apparently occasionally permissible not to bath your baby. On such occasions, a technical procedure known as topping and tailing would suffice. Topping and tailing? Who comes up with these names? And no, it has nothing to do with carrots or oral sex at all.

I was nervous at first, dithering a bit, constantly wanting to check the book to make sure I was doing it right, but I was immensely proud that I remembered how to do it: the bowl of cooled, boiled water for the eyes, the surgical spirits for the umbilical cord, all of it.

As I washed his tiny face (a fresh piece of cotton-wool for each eye), his pudgy little starfish hands, I found myself relaxing. It happened gradually, as I blew kisses on his tummy, snuggled my face into his sweet Elizabeth Anne's scented neck. I could see his big, serious eyes trying to focus on me and I was fascinated by this little boy, this tiny person who needed me so much, and whom I needed even more. I dressed him in his cuddly sleep suit (using them for real, at last!), then wrapped him in more blankets than were strictly necessary, and realised that it was done. I'd done it, all by myself, without mother or nurse or book, and he was still alive.

Oh, wonderful feeling! What an amazing sense of achievement, of competence, and totally unfamiliar, too. The tugging, stretching sensation of incredible, scary love growing stronger. It's like having a bubble inside your chest, a bubble that expands a little every day, catching you off guard sometimes, making you feel it might burst – like ***you*** might burst from happiness and love and contentment. As if you could ever have too much of those things. There is no better state of being in the world than this. I sat holding him in my arms for hours, talking, cuddling and just watching his face until he fell asleep. Yes, yes, I know you're not supposed to do this, but fuck it – wouldn't you?

I eventually relented and, with great ceremony, put my sleeping little angel to bed in his pram. Swaddled up cozily, lying on his side, blanket tucked behind him so he wouldn't roll onto his stomach or back and die of Sudden Infant Death Syndrome. I made a note of which side I'd put him down on, so that I could alternate sides to avoid the grossly misshapen flat head scenario. All as per spec. I was expecting him to wake up for a feed about three hours or so later, dreading the decision of whether or not to wake him, if he didn't stir of his own accord.

But three hours was a lifetime away. Right now, my concern was whether or not he was breathing. I checked and rechecked about a dozen times in the next couple of hours. I should have tried to sleep then, while I had the chance, but I was too wound up, almost hyperactive. I couldn't imagine how anybody could sleep at a time like this. To sleep would be to waste valuable baby-gazing time. I didn't want to let him out of my sight for a second, in case he stopped breathing, but mostly in case he disappeared while I was sleeping. In case some evil, reverse version of the baby-bringing stork dropped by to take him back where he really belonged. Metaphorically speaking, obviously. I knew perfectly well that storks didn't really bring babies. I was there, remember? I knew how he got out (and how he got ***in,*** not to put too fine a point on it).

But damn, was I ignorant. I want to laugh like a braying ass now, when I think of that silly girl who would give up precious, magical, beautiful sleep. That was the last time in my life I can remember feeling like that. From that night on, to this day, I'd give my left kidney for just twenty minutes of uninterrupted sleep. Jeez, I'd take ten minutes and throw in a chunk of my liver for free as well. Let me have a pillow and I swear you could take my corneas and I wouldn't even notice.

That night was endless. The Night of the Living Dead. He didn't wake up when he should have and I agonised for ages over whether to wake him or not. Eventually, I decided I had to – what if he starved to death in the night? Tried to wake him; he wasn't pleased. He wouldn't take the bottle. He didn't cry or make a fuss, he just refused to drink. Tried everything – warm milk, room temperature milk, different teats. Nothing. He just became increasingly annoyed. And I became increasingly panicked. My mother tried (maybe he feels you're getting tense? Grrrr). I tried again. He was having none of it. Gave up on the bottle and tried a medicine dropper, then a teaspoon. Drip, drool, wipe, grizzle. One millilitre at a time. Do you know how much a millilitre actually is? It's a vast, absurd volume of liquid. Do you know how long it takes to get one measly 50ml feed down the throat of an angry newborn? It takes a very long time, let me tell you. About two hours and four cups of coffee, to be precise.

The procedure was repeated twice during the night, and once again in the early morning. Poor child. I should have left him to sleep. Trust me to try and do things by the book – the really ancient, out-of-date Old-Wiveish book, too. The nurses at the hospital had told me 50ml every three hours and, by God, there'd be no deviating from instructions.

It's all about Routine, you see. You gotta establish a routine, or else you're screwed. Or so they'd have us believe. If anybody had told me then that babies know when they're hungry and will not let themselves starve – I would have laughed in their faces. I know this ***now*** – I have a deliciously healthy, demand-fed second child to prove it. But this knowledge was still years away. I struggled through the night, my mother sitting up with me, both of us taking turns with the dropper, me crying, pleading with him to ***please just swallow a little***. It was awful. Would it always be like this? I felt sick at the thought.

It did get better. As soon as my mother and I returned from a teat-buying spree. We were convinced he didn't like the ones we had and would drink better if only we could find the perfect nipple-replacement. And we did. That afternoon Steven gulped his feeds down like a baby starved. We were excited, but felt guilty, too, at how stupid we'd been, using those cheap-shit teats and depriving him of nourishment.

At last he was taking milk – I wasn't a dismal failure of a mother, he wouldn't die, I wouldn't go to jail for child neglect. Oh happy day.

Just a pity we didn't pay more attention to the small print on the teat packaging. The tiny print that read, "Cereal Teat". It was only a few days later that we discovered the giant, x-shaped holes the size of ten-cent pieces in these teats, designed to feed runny cereal through a bottle (who the hell would do that?). Steven wasn't guzzling down his milk because he was starving hungry – he was just trying not to drown!

The first weeks passed in a blur of sleep deprivation, Steri-Nappi and marathon sessions of gooey-eyed baby-gazing. I wasn't one of those mothers who'd put baby down in his bouncy chair and get on with fabulous yummy-mummy things like pedicures and lunch with the girls, as in, "the baby is going to fit into ***my*** lifestyle**...** Bloody ha ha, by the way. That's just something ***Marie Claire*** invented to make us dowdy mothers feel bad about ourselves and thus prompt us to buy more magazines that would tell us which lipstick would solve all our problems.

Besides, I didn't ***have*** a lifestyle before Steven came along. Now I did, but it didn't involve much lipstick. My new lifestyle was one of unwashed hair and pyjamas at two in the afternoon. But I loved it. I loved every minute of it, even the hard days when he seemed grumpy and I couldn't understand what he wanted. Even on the days I was so tired I couldn't see straight by lunchtime. I held him ninety percent of the time in those first weeks, even when he was sleeping. Shooting myself in the foot completely when, later on, he wouldn't go to sleep by himself. But it made me happy.

Poor little Maria didn't get the same treatment when she was a newborn. I was cured of my OCD baby-holding by then, and was even capable of going to the toilet without taking her with me, an unthinkable lapse in Steven's baby days. Thinking back now, I'm sad to realise that some of the details have faded in my memory over the years. Back then, I was so sure I'd remember every second forever. But then you wake up one day and realise you can't remember the name of your first real boyfriend, but you do know all the words to every song Barney ever sang. Stuff like that could depress a girl.

What does stick in my mind about those first months is yoghurt. Lots and lots of yoghurt. It was the only thing I could eat. I couldn't face the thought of any other food. Suppertime was especially hard, with its awful smells of frying onions and grilled chicken. It was almost as bad as morning sickness, though caused by something entirely different – adrenalin and nerves. I became wonderfully skinny, but I was way too busy, tired and consumed by motherly devotion to notice or care. (The skinny thing didn't last, by the way, which is not really surprising. The phase passed only too quickly and I was soon back to my normal macaroni-cheese-scoffing, chunky self.)

There is no end to the ways in which parents can get things horribly wrong. And you don't have to try very hard. Even when you think you're doing it right, you probably aren't.

Like the day I gave Steven his first proper bath – an incident we still laugh about (well, ***I*** don't find it that funny, personally). The poor baby started yelling and squirming in the bath and I couldn't figure out why. I checked the water temperature (for the fifth time, with both elbows, wrists and probably my tongue as well), I checked for nappy rash (no chance of that, his nappy was changed roughly every fifteen minutes, whether or not he thought of weeing in it), I searched for pin pricks (even though I used one of those Snappi things and not a safety pin). Then I noticed the colour of his arm. And not a moment too soon – it was probably about to fall off. That corpsy shade of bluish-purple scared me so much I very nearly ***did*** drop him in the water. In my zeal, I'd held his arm too tightly. Then, in my fluster, I managed to get soap on his hands which he rubbed into his eyes. Goddammit. Don't you know you're not supposed to soap baby's hands? Didn't you read the books? They're very clear on this point. Next thing you'll be feeding him Sto-pain intravenously – and then you're one step away from those mothers who let their children run with scissors. Call yourself a mother? Sheesh.

This was a new voice in my head, a new incarnation of Sensible Tracy, but more like Sensible-Tracy-On-Crack, perhaps. Sensible-Gone-Psycho. Sensible Tracy from the Seventh Circle of Hell. I think she came standard with my brand new guilt gland. Sensible-Gone-Psycho's job is to make me doubt myself. She's the evil little demon sitting on my shoulder, whispering how pathetic I am – 24/7.

She knows all the tricks, and she's sneaky. She disguises herself as the Voice of Good Motherliness, but she ***lies***. She convinces me I can't have the things I want, she shouts at me when I get things wrong, she tells me I don't deserve to be happy. I've taken to calling her Sister Tracy, because she has the shrill nails-on-a-blackboard voice of a nun I once knew. She's settled in very comfortably over the years, and these days it seems she's pretty much in charge. Not so healthy. I need to kill her off, but I don’t know how. I’m thinking arsenic. Or a stake through the heart. Seriously, that bitch must die.

Chapter Seven

1994 – 1995: In which she goes postal and to the ball

Against all odds, despite that Satanic nun in my head, I managed to learn which way was up. In just a few, short weeks I went from incompetent hell-mother to semi-capable Steven expert. I gained confidence. Things that seemed intimidating in the beginning became second nature to me. The scariest thing wasn't the physical aspect of looking after him – I soon realised he wasn't as fragile as he looked and I actually ***was*** capable of feeding, bathing and dressing him without causing any lasting damage. It wasn't even the sheer mind-blowing bizarreness of knowing that I loved someone more than I thought humanly possible, without being a stalker.

No. The most frightening part of it all was making the ***decisions.*** That daunting question that demands an answer a thousand times a day: What now?

Dr Spock and Supernanny are all good and well, and they know their stuff, to be sure. However. They are not in the room when your baby goes to sleep ten minutes before you were going to bath him, for example. Nobody is there to tell you whether you should just let him sleep in his dirty clothes and wet nappy, or wake him and risk trying to bath a screechy, slippery bundle of infant fury, then struggle for five hours to get him back to sleep afterwards. What do you do? What do you do if he doesn't finish his bottle for the third time in a row? Is he terribly ill? Is he just not hungry today? Is he thirsty perhaps? Should I give him some water instead? This book says he can have water, that one says under no circumstances. What if he gets constipated? Or diarrhoea? Is this bit supposed to be that colour? Has the rash got better or worse since we changed the washing powder? Oh my God, is it ***meningitis?!***

How am I supposed to know what to do? The feeling of abject incompetence, while bluffing for the camera, is the loneliest feeling in the world. You think you're the only one who has no idea what she's doing, and nobody ever tells you they felt the same way. You have a helpless little person entirely dependant on you and your ability to make the right decisions – to ***know*** what decision to make. The pressure is relentless, the constant uncertainty enough to dissolve even the most together mother into a gooey puddle of ***snot en trane.***

But I did it. Somehow. I'm still doing it today. And with each new situation, I'm still utterly clueless. I've made hundreds of mistakes (no, I'm not telling), and I'm sure to make plenty more. Hopefully they won't be big. Okay, maybe one or two big ones. (Talk to Steven's therapist in twenty years and he should be able to tell you how badly I've screwed up.) In the process, I've learned a trick or two.

Trick number one: if you're worrying about whether you're doing it right, you're on the right track. You can always tell the parents who believe they're doing a fantastic job. They're the ones whose children torture small, fluffy creatures. Sure, the guilt and the voracious monster fear of ruining your child for life gnaws away at your soul until there's nothing left but a desolate windswept vacuum, but at least it keeps you honest, right? Right?

Trick number two is the easiest way to check your parental aptitude: how many times have you dropped your child on the head? More than twice and you're probably screwed. Less than that, you might be okay. Watch for puppy-kicking. Quite simple, really.

Great parenting in two easy steps.

Sooner than I would have thought possible, the day came that I realised I knew my baby better than anyone else. I could comfort him better than anyone, and I was his favourite person in the world. It happens to all mothers. I just didn't expect it to happen to me.

My life had taken on a routine of mothering, studying, more mothering, compulsive yawning. I was tired all the time. By early afternoon, I'd be barely conscious, operating entirely on autopilot. Steven had heard about sleeping through the night, but this was apparently something that happened to other people. He didn't see how it applied to him. His daytime naps were short, not long enough to make a snack ***and*** sleep, for example – you had to choose. Eat or sleep? Hmmm… dumb question.

Steven was healthy, a sturdy, happy baby who had my whole family wrapped around his chunky little finger. I remember the sheer joy of watching him grow and learn, reaching each milestone on target, or even earlier. The angst-ridden excitement of each new stage, like starting him on solids (apples and pears were his favourite. ***Do not*** try the fish and veg variety. Trust me, it's cat food in a jar. And strained carrots lead to alarmingly orange nappies, which is not a sign of cancer, so don't stress. I couldn't wait for him to reach the third stage of Purity – those banana and caramel puddings looked so good. And while we're on the topic: jelly sniffed up your baby's nose ***will*** melt eventually, and does not pose any threat of suffocation. Don't panic. Just laugh. Okay, panic a little first. Then laugh.)

Mom was a huge help – she took care of Steven every morning while I studied. Or rather, while I sat at my desk and stared uncomprehendingly at my books, drooling a little. It was hard getting back into the work. My mind was on Steven constantly, and every squeak or cry I heard had me rushing out of my room to see what was up.

Some mornings, I never even made it to my desk. My mom and I would sit in the lounge, drinking gallons of tea and discussing our favourite subject – Steven. We'd analyse his bowel movements, possible teething and strategies for getting him to sleep just five minutes longer. And gushing. We gushed a lot. He was so perfect, so strong and healthy, much more beautiful than any other baby we'd ever seen, of course.

Those mornings brought my mother and me so close. It was wonderful to have someone to share it with, someone who actually got it, and wasn't just listening to be polite, while furtively scanning the room for a gun to blow their heads off. I've seen that glazed look in people's eyes when I talk about my children. At first

I felt bad about it, all awkward and embarrassed to be boring them. Not anymore. These days my approach is: I'll gush if I want and you just try and stop me. If you don't like it, please feel free to bugger off. Hey, two times natural childbirth with zero painkillers – I've earned my bragging rights, I'd say. I reckon all mothers should be permitted a certain amount of free swanking about our offspring.

Parental swank should be legalised, of course. But until then, allow me to offer some tips to ensure that you still have one or two friends left by the time your child is out of nappies.

Slightly Yummy Mummy's Guide to Getting Your Gush On While Steering Clear of Social Suicide

Tip #1 Be cool when talking to other parents. Of course it's obvious that your baby is the most beautiful, most talented, most intelligent child to ever walk the earth. I know this and you know this – but be aware that every parent believes this about their own children. It's bad form to argue, so just indulge them. With a perfect child such as your own, you can afford to be magnanimous. Listen to their unlikely stories of how Caitlin (terrible name that, almost as bad as Chelsea) slept through from birth and little Joshua's advanced speech development. It's only polite. They should do the same for you.

Tip #2 Among other parents, it's sometimes a good idea to downplay your own child's prodigious achievements, while enthusiastically mooing about Joshua/Caitlin's nonsensical gabbling. This is quite important. Lie if you have to. Whatever you do, for God's sake, do not point out to Joshua's/Caitlin's mother that ***your*** child was using two word sentences at that age. This will only piss her off. In extreme cases, bring out the big guns and talk about how worried you are about your child's delayed crawling/lactose intolerance/refusal to eat anything other than Flings. This will leave the other parent with a warm, fuzzy feeling of parental superiority, which should surely earn you another invitation to tea and cake. But beware. This could easily turn into a deadly game of My Life Sucks More Than Yours. Pitfalls abound as you try to convince your mothers' group that you have it so much worse than them. They might cluck sympathetically at your dilemmas while feeling better about themselves (10 points); they could start slipping you pamphlets about postnatal depression or special needs children (0 points), or they could turn on you completely for being a whiny, neurotic, self-absorbed cow (-100 points and definitely no more coffee mornings).

Tip #3 When talking to childless friends, you are permitted to boast with impunity. Two reasons: you're not going to offend them by implying your child is better than theirs and, more importantly, they don't know any better. For all they know, it truly ***is*** miraculous for a baby to be able to pick up a single Rice Krispie using the two-fingered pincer grip at only six-and-a-half months. The obvious downside here is that they might not give a shit. They might find this whole baby thing terribly dull and start avoiding you anyway. Take time to decide whether you care or not.

Tip #4 A quick word about that other category: Childless People With Dogs. Not just any people with dogs, but Dog People, you understand. There's just no reasoning with this sort. Their dogs are their babies and they truly believe it's the same thing. My advice is, back away slowly while smiling and nodding, and you might get out of there alive. You will feel the urge to grab their shoulders and shake them, yelling, "It's a DOG for God's sake! It is not a human! It's a fucking DOG! What's the matter with you, can't you see that?" ***Do not succumb***. You're better than that. Just leave them to their delusion and be on your way. Okay, bring on the hate-mail from the Corgi Club, but let me just say this – I happen to like dogs. Dogs are nice. My doggy is part of my family, while remaining… a dog. It seems obvious to me, but then, I'm not a Dog Person. Clearly I must be missing the point. (Just realised I'm not really a People Person either. Maybe I should take up gardening.)

***

At some point, I stopped consciously thinking of myself as "the pregnant girl", and simply became a mom. I don't know exactly when that happened, or how. Just by living it every day, I suppose. I know it took others longer to see me the way I saw myself. To some people I was still "that girl", and Steven wasn't a real boy, he was still "The Situation". It irritated me more than it should have – I've always taken things very personally and, dammit, I want people to ***like*** me. I needed others to see us the way

I did – an ordinary mother and child, mom doing her best, bumbling through like anyone else and getting it right, mostly.

I wanted them to see Steven as the blessing that he was – not a burden, not a mistake, not a Situation. Meant to be. Beyond responsibility, I ***wanted*** to do my best for him, to be the best mother I could be. I think I've done a good job so far, even though sometimes I don't know whether it's been good enough. For one thing, I didn't give him the father he deserved.

I don't know how David felt about Steven back then. Did he care about him and not know how to show it? Was he scared and intimidated? When he thought of his son (if he did), what did he feel? Guilt, confusion, any love at all? Did he think it was too late to make it right? I didn't understand then, and I still don't. But it's not for me to understand anymore. It's between Steven and his father. In some ways that's a relief, but it's also scary to let it go. It's hard to accept that it's out of my hands now. I'm standing back, leaving my child vulnerable, maybe letting him get hurt, and I can only stand by and watch. It's the hardest thing I've ever done, and I still don't know if it's the right thing.

David visited us in the hospital. He held Steven, brought a present, gave me a hug and went home again. In the very early weeks, he visited fairly often. A few times, for short periods, I attempted to leave father and son alone together, but it was never long before David would call me back in a panic.

Maybe I was expecting too much, maybe my frantic demands for any sign of fatherly love freaked him out. As the weeks went by, David's visits became more erratic, promises were made and broken, and very little in the way of maintenance or support was offered. It made me angry, mother-bear-like, and mean. It made me sad, too, but my maternal instincts kicked in and the sadness was channelled into handy head-exploding aggression. Excellent.

I remember Sunday evenings spent watching the road, waiting to spot his car approaching. That was supposed to be visiting time, but he hardly ever came. Even though Steven was much too young to understand, each disappointment ate at my guts like battery acid. I was angry for Steven's sake, heartbroken for his sake that his father didn't care enough. To me, that's what it came down to – he didn't care enough about his child to be there for him when he said he would. I saw him occasionally with his friends or girlfriend. Partying, drinking, doing nineteen-year-old stuff. Except he wasn't a typical nineteen-year-old any more than I was a typical fifteen-year-old. We were different. I'd accepted that. Why wouldn't he?

I rarely mentioned money or maintenance. He was a student and I understood that he didn't have lot of money. And he did bring clothes and toiletries a few times. Cotton-wool balls spring to mind. I like to think I was reasonable on that issue. In fact, I took great pains to be reasonable, so that nobody could ever accuse me of being the money-grubbing ex (at the age of fifteen!).

I wasn't angry about all the responsibility resting on my shoulders. I didn't want or need him to help me. All I wanted from him was to be a dad to his child. I don't think he understood that part. Maybe he (and his family) thought I wanted something more, something for myself. I didn't. I had the support of my own family. Not to mention the merry little band of alternate personalities in my head cheering me on (or bringing me down). I had my rigid self-discipline to fall back on when I felt shaky.

I didn't need David. But Steven did. And still does.

I tried so hard to make David see that – too hard. So hard that when he did visit occasionally, we'd always end up fighting. I'd accuse him of being a terrible father, lecture him for being late, skipping visits or not phoning often enough. Realising I wasn't getting through to him, I'd freak and became even more hostile. He'd get all defensive and we'd end up in I-Said-And-Then-You-Said fights. Never productive.

Still, for someone who doesn't generally do confrontation, I managed to make myself heard. By the neighbours, too. That would be the night I chased after him when he left in a huff. That was the beginning of the end and I cringe when I think of it. I did everything wrong. (Guilt gland ticking over briskly.) I can't help wondering how it might have been if I hadn't lost my temper that night. Would David have stuck around? Would Steven have known his father all these years? The what-ifs keep me awake at night.

The fight probably started with those infamous words, "We need to talk". Jeez, how many times have I said that in my life? No good ever comes of it, let me tell you. It started off as a standard David/Tracy conversation, but went downhill fast.

Tracy (grimfaced, holding baby in arms): "We need to talk."

David (warily – he's been here before): "Yes?"

Tracy (steam visibly beginning to escape from ears): "You said you'd be here at six. It's after seven."

David (doesn't get the big deal): "Yeah, I'm sorry, hey! Couldn't be helped. It won't happen again, okay?"

Tracy (cheeks all red and blotchy, fists clenched, top of head unscrewing): "That's what you said last time. And last week? Where were you? Something better come up? Did your child just slip your mind again? You can't keep doing this, David. Steven needs you. When are you going to grow up?"

And so it went. Accusation and denial, sarcasm and defensiveness. The usual formula. Only, this time I lost it. I went psycho fishwife on his ass. You should have seen me.

"You don't deserve to be his father!" I yelled at him. "Steven deserves so much better than you!" I was still holding Steven (holding my child while shouting at his father. Lovely, hey? Somebody, give the woman some curlers and a cigarette. I could be on ***My Name Is Earl***).

I'd pushed him too far.

"I don't have to take this from you!" he said, angry now. Usually, he just stood there and took it, mumbling the occasional apology. Not this time. He stormed past me, out of Steven's bedroom, and I chased after him, stopping only to put Steven down on the couch. He was so little, still swaddled in a blanket. I wonder sometimes if he has any memory of that night.

"Where are you going? Running away again?" I shouted from the doorway. He was halfway up the steps and nearly gone. I thought if I let him leave now, Steven would lose his dad forever. So I followed him out onto the pavement, and there we stood yelling at each other like Jerry Springer people. Not my finest moment.

But it made no difference. He left and didn't come back for a long time.

Whenever he did, eventually, it never lasted. The gaps between visits and phone calls would become longer and longer, and eventually stop altogether. For a while. Then the whole cycle would start over, governed, perhaps, by David's own guilt gland. I was always so grateful when he did come back, that while he behaved, I'd forget to be angry. I gave him a thousand second chances, because I didn't want to be the one who denied Steven the father he needed.

But even a thousand second chances run out sooner or later. Then you have to make a decision.

Around the time of Steven's first birthday, David announced that he was going to live in Durban with his dad. I became angry all over again. It seemed like he'd finally hatched a plan to escape his responsibilities – to do a runner. At last, the easy way out had presented itself and he grabbed it with both hands. Or so it seemed to me. He left, and for ages I heard nothing from him.

I'd like to think it must have been hard for him, too; he's not a bad guy.

In the end, I think it just became easier to stay away. Once you've let things get so bad, maybe you can't see a way back. Maybe he thought I hated him. Maybe he didn't understand what I wanted from him. Maybe he didn't know how. I can say "maybe" until monkeys fly out of my butt – the truth is, David stuffed up. He had a job to do and he didn't do it. Now, nearly twelve years later, he has a son who lives on the other side of the world, a son he doesn't know – not really. Not the way a father knows his child. I can't imagine how hard that must be to live with.

Out of the blue, on his second birthday, Steven received a birthday card from David. I will never forget that card. I was so hopeful when I read those words:

Dearest Steven,

Happy Birthday. I will send a present and a letter soon.

Lots of love, from Daddy

Five months went by with no letter, no present, no phone call from Daddy. Hope turned to disappointment, then to anger, and finally to cold, implacable resolve. He'd gone too far. You don't make promises like that to a child if you have no intention of keeping them. That's how children are broken – and there was no way I'd let my child be broken. I waited for something throughout those five months – I had to be sure. I also had to wait until most of the anger was gone.

Then I wrote a letter of my own. Written on lined exam pad paper in my scratchy seventeen-year-old handwriting, it was a polite, mature letter – not nasty, but very clear. When I posted the letter, I felt it slip from my fingers into the dark post-box slot. It felt so damn ***final.*** I cried as I wrote it, and I cried as I posted it. It must have arrived in Durban a real mess, a soggy, tear-stained Get-Out-Of-Jail-Free card.

What I'd written was that if he couldn't be a proper father to Steven, then it was best if he stayed away. I told him that having ***no*** father was better than having a ***lousy*** father who hurt and disappointed his child, a father who wasn't strong enough to stand up and take responsibility. I told him that Steven only needed people in his life who would be there for him one hundred percent. I told him to go, and not come back.

And he did. I didn't hear from him again for seven years.

If he had fought for Steven, even if he had begged for another of those thousand second chances, I would have given in. This wasn't the way I wanted it. I didn't want to explain to Steven that he didn't have a daddy because mommy sent him away. That would be bad. But worse would be watching him swallow that daily dose of slow-acting poison: ***Maybe my daddy will remember me today.***

I was trying to protect my boy, that's all. Whether that was the right decision – well, I guess Steven has to decide that for himself.

Sigh… this is depressing.

Meanwhile, life carried on. I saw some of my old friends occasionally, but I didn't go out much. That was okay with me. I hadn't given dating a thought. If I had, the thought would probably have been "Oh God, does that mean I'll have to shave my legs?"

When Steven was ten months old, my friend Bianca invited me to a Valentine's Ball at her school. I was to fill in as a partner for a friend whose date couldn't make it. She phoned me the day before (me being the only person she knew who'd definitely be home on a Saturday night) and said, "Hello darling. I'm afraid I've got you in the soup." Bianca says things like that.

I was reluctant at first (babysitting arrangements, leg-shaving issue, complete lack of any social skills whatsoever), but she managed to twist my rubber arm and off I went. I got myself all dollied-up for the first time in a year-and-a-half, and was surprised to discover that I still remembered what lipstick was for. I felt strange among all those school kids. They were all so different from me. But it was somewhat exciting, too – the glamorous single mother out on the town, devastating the admiring plebs with her wit and awe-inspiring maturity. Yeah, right. I was jelly-kneed and tongue-tied all night.

We met my date, James, at the school. He was late and I was starting to think I'd been stood up. But then he arrived – handsome, smelling good, tall and serious. Four of my top five requirements in a man, in no particular order. Absolute obedience to my every whim can wait until the third date – nobody could ever call me unreasonably demanding.

This wasn't the first time I'd met him. We'd been introduced a few months earlier in front of the local Steers (sadly, it's no longer there. Many a long Friday night was spent there, ten of us lingering for five hours over two plates of chips and half a glass of water). I was with Bianca, enjoying one of my very rare nights out. She knew him from work.

I can still see him standing there in the parking lot across from his flat, wearing blue and white striped boxers, socks with no shoes, no shirt, a beer in his hand.

"Good evening, ladies," he'd said in a quiet drawl I found appealing. That, for the record, was the first time I met James. Even if he doesn't remember, I do.

He was cute. I liked his confidence, his sleepy-eyed charm – his ***adultness.*** This here was no boy, and I liked that.

He looked so good the night of the dance. I was shy and awkward, but compensated by being just a little bit slutty. I'd like to say I was a bold, confident young woman going for what she wanted, but I think slutty would be more accurate. Such a fine line there. It's hard to get the balance right. Err on the side of caution and you'll die a shrivelled old maid. Err on the side of ***Cosmo*** and you might just die a whole lot sooner, shrivelling and oozing optional. Yuck.

We danced and we laughed, we spoke about Steven, we kissed. Alright, I kissed him. He was a little taken aback, but dammit, a girl's gotta do what a girl's gotta do. Can't be hanging around forever waiting for demure, gentlemanly types to get their act together. Carpe Diem and all that, right? More like Carpe My Only Chance Of Getting Laid Anytime Before Menopause!

I had a lovely time, and after much deliberation, I saw him again the following night. A late Valentine rose was delivered to my house with a card that read, "Would you be my Valentine? Love, James".

Melt…

As it turned out, I would certainly be his Valentine. Within a few weeks, I was his girlfriend, too.

Scary stuff, considering Steven. But the two of them clicked immediately. James accepted Steven completely and that nasty boyfriend vs child tug-of-war never happened. He came to love Steven as his own child. That sort of thing doesn't come around very often and I was lucky that my first, tentative foray into dating as a single mother was with someone like him. He was just what I needed then – a family man with a five-year-plan. He was reliable and responsible – a nice young man whom I could happily take home to Mom. Like me, he wanted the white picket fence and a happy family (possibly, I suspect, the Stepford wife, too, but that's a whole different chapter). He showed me what was possible for me, and I'm grateful for that.

Unfortunately, he also ruined me for future relationships. Ever since, I've compared my boyfriends' interaction with Steven with his, and they always seem to come up short. So far.

Chapter Eight

In which she remains stubbornly unsaved

Then I blinked and Steven was nearly three years old.

How does that happen? What happens to all those cute, drooling bundles that hang around their prams, doing little more than generate tons of dirty nappies? Where did this other boy come from – this wide-eyed, serious child who could name every internal organ at two and write his name at three? Steven was a sensitive soul who scared me sometimes – if you think a newborn is intimidating, try spending five minutes with a three-year-old whose favourite word is "Why". You will feel a strong urge to run away screaming, as your brain liquefies and dribbles out of your ears. The boiling point of human brain matter, it turns out, is the approximately twenty-second repeat rate of the question "Why?" in any given conversation.

I realised with a shock one day that he was no longer a mewling, leaky pudding relying on me simply for physical survival. Here was an intelligent, real person, who required far more complicated actions than handiness with a Wet Wipe.

"Ho, ho! You poor, naive sap," jeers Future Tracy. "Try being a single mother to a moody, silent twelve-year-old boy! Ain't nobody else gonna talk Erections 101, darlin'. It's all on you. You'll be begging to explain the Jesus/aliens/Father Christmas connection instead."

Babies don't come with a manual. Everybody knows that. But when you come right down to it, really, one baby is pretty much like another. They eat, they sleep, they cry, they poo. And then they do it all again. Your job is to make sure the proportions are correct. It's not that complicated. I don't mean to burst your comfy bubble, but it's true. Once you get the hang of it, babies are ***easy.*** Don't look at me like that – I know all about colic and sleepless nights. Hard work, for sure. But easy to understand – eat-sleep-cry-poo. Figure out which goes where and you've got it waxed.

There are many reasons why babies are preferable to later models:

They don't end every conversation with, "I hate you!" and a head-splitting door slam.

They don't talk back and confuse you with cunning arguments.

They don't ask difficult religious questions.

They don't demand Liquorice Allsorts for supper.

Any dumbass with a boob and a goodly supply of Pampers can get by just fine. But try telling that to the mother of a newborn. You're likely to get yelled at and cried on.

Then, just as you think you're getting the hang of this baby thing, the little horrors turn on you. At roughly three years of age, everything changes – cuteness levels drop and continue to do so until the age of twelve, when any remaining cuteness is shed in favour of monosyllabic surliness. Baby books should, at this stage, be replaced by The Art of War and perhaps selected works by Machiavelli. Forget ***Chicken Souping*** your way through it. You'll need less of the Gratitude Journal and more of the Jedi Mind Trick. What we need is a parenting book written by Yoda: "Grounded, you are. To your room, go you will."

I like that.

But at three? If a manual existed for three-year-olds like Steven, it would have to be the one translated into English from Chinese by a committee of dyslexic Norwegians, remaindered in Sudan and burned as fuel to boil water – impossible to come by. He wasn't your average gooey-nose-picking sweetie-gobbler. For Steven, getting his hands sticky was a major catastrophe. Likewise if two different food types touched each other on his plate (did I mention the OCD factor?). Clothes and shoe shopping was a nightmare – scratchy labels had to be removed immediately upon purchase and much of the coolest stuff avoided because it wasn't "comfy". He's like that to this day. Fashion is not on his radar. Never mind fashion, it's hard enough getting him to wear pants without holes in them. Some day, when you're not looking, my son, those damn fluffy dishwater-coloured tracksuit pants are going to fall prey to a mysterious washing line thief. Or something.

In 1997, the concept of twelve years old didn't exist for me. Wet dreams, girl trouble and long division were all so far in the future, I could safely ignore them for now. Three years was momentous enough for me, angelic baby and chubby toddler things of the past, nappies and bottles a distant memory. On his way to being – gasp – a preschooler.

Preschool! I was excited. A whole new world of learning and playing and friends would open up for Steven. I pictured packing healthy lunches – muffins, carrot sticks and elaborate sandwiches. I saw him kissing me goodbye in the morning, happily skipping off to play with his friends in the sandpit. I imagined finger paintings on the fridge, the wheels on the bus going round and round, sweet, rosy-cheeked teachers reading stories on the mat. It was going to be so much fun.

Oh, what was that? Did you hear that ominous roll of thunder and the howl of the eldritch wolf? Again? Oh yeah. I should have known.

When it came to preschools, there wasn't a whole lot of choice. I avoided the most obviously dodgy playschools advertised in the local paper – those run by hard-faced, chain-smoking women in ski-pants and the one where misbehaving children were rumoured to be locked in the toilet. Besides those, the preschools in the area were all run on Sound Christian Principles, which, by the way, doesn't really mean Love Thy Neighbour and Jesus Loves Me and All Things Bright and Beautiful. Surprising, isn't it? Beat Children Into Submission While Brainwashing With Cultish Dogma would be more accurate. I sure was shocked. Unfortunately, by the time I figured this out, my poor little boy was in the clutches of the born-again crazies and it took some ugly scenes to get him out.

The first school I went to see was a definite no. I considered it because it was one of the few with no religious reference in the name. I thought this indicated some inclination towards moderation and non-fanaticism. Silly me.

I was impressed at first. Dozens of quiet, well-behaved little children marched into the classroom in single file, all wearing identical plastic aprons. All seemed organised and well-established. Pleasant outside area, with bikes and toys in pristine condition. James and I smiled hopefully at each other – this seemed promising. (Yes, he tagged along, looking and sounding serious with his navy pullover and pertinent questions. We'd been together almost two years by then, and I was sporting a semi-engagement ring. I was ever so proud of my ring, even though I strongly suspected it had been recycled from a previous girlfriend).

My first impression of the principal was good. She looked like a comfy granny, all floral blouse and Estée Lauder. As she showed us around, once again I was struck by how tidy it was, and how quiet. Too quiet... A little warning bell began to ring, but I shushed it. What did I know about preschools anyway? These were professionals. Who was I to question? Meanwhile, Steven had formed his own opinion – and he was not amused.

He clung to my leg like a limpet and refused to let go, no matter how I coaxed, begged, ordered or contorted my body in the hope of dislodging him. I smiled sheepishly at Principal Grandma as I tried to peel him off, so that I could read the indemnity form like the proper grown-up I was trying to be. I expected to see her smiling indulgently back at me: Don't worry, I see this all the time, it's quite normal.

That's not what I got.

Her lips pulled into a thin line, and she said in her best stepmotherly voice, "You need to put that child down now."

Good grief. Nobody had ever called my boy That Child before. I was taken aback, but pressed on with my list of questions.

"So… um… how do you handle discipline here?" I asked in my best excuse-me-for-breathing voice.

This time, the indulgent smile did appear as she chuckled, "We find we don't have too many discipline problems here. I've been in this business for a long time and I know how to handle the little buggers."

Did she just call the children buggers? Alarms screeching now. Warning! Warning! Red Alert, Defcon 1, self-destruct imminent… Yet I stood and listened.

"I had problems with a boy in my class last year who was exposing himself to the other children…" she continued.

Oh my. There's just no good ending to that sentence. My expression of polite interest froze in place and my eyes glazed over as I waited for the undoubtedly disturbing punchline.

Chuckle, chuckle again. This lady was rather impressed with herself, you could tell.

"Yes, I handled it quite well. I just told him his ***tollie*** would fall off and the dogs would eat it if he did it again. He's kept his pants on ever since. His mother thought it was a wonderful idea."

I'm sure she did, you bitch! That's because she's obviously crazy, too. She'd have to be to send her child here. What is it with all these creepy people in my story?

This was clearly not the place for Steven. Not even close. I felt so sorry for the children stuck there. I wanted to open the front gate and help them escape to freedom, like a Greenpeacer let loose in a vivisection lab. Run little ones! Run while you can! Of course I did no such thing.

We left Auntie Cruella, ***tollies*** intact, but illusions shattered. I wonder how many innocent kids she's bullied into chronic adolescent bedwetting. It's a sad thought. Finding a preschool was proving to be not as easy or as much fun as I'd imagined.

Our nerves fragile and optimism greatly reduced, we moved on to the next place on my list. Noisier, less tidy, a nicer looking principal. The children seemed to like her. I saw lots of them skipping up to her for hugs. Stockholm Syndrome, I realise now.

When I asked my discipline question, cleverly mentioning smacking specifically, she seemed shocked.

"Oh no, we ***never*** smack the children. Good heavens! Definitely not."

Such an open, ingenuous face. She looked absolutely horrified that I could suggest such a thing.

At last, a likely option. This little school seemed to have it all – friendly teachers, finger paintings, dog-eared books, mess and noise. All strong indicators that learning was taking place. And I liked her. I admit it, I was taken in. She was younger and snazzier than the other teachers I'd seen, and although she mentioned, too casually, her Christian Principles, I believed it would be okay. Surely, the whole point of Christianity was basically to be nice to others? What's wrong with children learning that? Nothing, as far as I could see. So I could easily overlook my slight unease at the join-the-dots crucifixion pictures.

As we left, application form in hand, I heard the soggy, heart-warming tones of twenty three-year-olds singing ***The Wheels on the Bus***, accompanied by postnasal drip. Nobody could remember what the Grannies on the Bus did, but that's hardly the point, is it?

First day of school. Scared as hell. Lots of tears. And that was just me.

Steven's little brown suitcase was packed with spare clothes, fruit, notebook for the teacher to write sweet, encouraging notes in (so I imagined).

I'd been preparing him for this day for weeks and I thought we were ready. He seemed excited. As we went inside, he went off to play immediately, which encouraged me. I chatted briefly to his teacher. Miss Timid was a soft-spoken lady with frantic eyes, who was obviously out of her depth and actually looked like she could snap at any moment. She assured me he'd be okay. He was happy enough as I hugged him and left him playing with blocks. I wasn't sure if he understood that I was leaving him there, but it was too late to turn back now. I left quickly, before I could change my mind.

On my way out, I peeked through the window – he looked so cute and grown up. I cried again. It was exciting and scary and sad, all at the same time. My boy was growing up.

I watched the clock all morning, drinking gallons of coffee and pacing the house. God, what a long day. Mom and I barely spoke. We didn't have to. We knew. Three more hours… two more hours…

We gave in eventually and arrived to fetch him a ridiculous forty-five minutes early, waiting outside and feeling sheepish, but we didn't care. Do you know how long forty-five minutes is? We waited a decade or two, then I hurried inside, only to find his classroom empty.

Nobody in sight. God! Oh God, where have they taken him? It's crazy how many thoughts can go through your head in ten seconds.

Then I heard it – the sound of Steven (and a dozen other children) crying inconsolably. I followed the sound to the lunchroom, which was in chaos. Miss Timid was holding Steven and absently jiggling him on her hip, while trying to control twenty other, sobbing, fighting, food-throwing darlings. I was shocked. Surely, this wasn't how it's supposed to be?

I should have taken him away, there and then, never to come back. He seemed traumatised the whole afternoon and didn't want to talk about his day. I wanted to hear about sandpits and finger painting and story circles. I needed to hear that he was okay, that I hadn't made a dreadful mistake. Instead, I realised he'd spent the whole day crying in the corner. He hated me for abandoning him, I just knew it.

The second day was much, much worse. He knew what would happen when I said goodbye. I felt like the worst mother in the world, peeling him off me and walking away. Jeez. I must have been loony. I wish I could be one of those bossy, overbearing parents who pushed everyone around and annoy teachers with their demands. I'm just too nice, too much of a wuss.

Only much later did I come to know what the teachers there were really like and how they'd lied straight to my face when telling me how the school was run. Christian values, indeed. They seemed to favour all the best bits of the Old Testament, if you ask me. Lots of sparing-the-rod-and-spoiling-the-child type advice.

The school was run by Tweedle-Dumb, the principal, and her best friend, Tweedle-Dumber. Both were nasty, small-minded and ignorant, with a pair of giant egos to match. Neither seemed to like children much. But boy, could they act! Academy Awards all round for their roles as caring, intelligent human beings.

Miss Timid was a bit of an outsider. She was sweeter than the two Tweedles, who ganged up on her. Much later, I heard them undermining her in front of the children and complaining about her to the parents. In the early days, of course, I didn't know any of this. I was completely fooled. I thought they cared. I confided in them about My Situation. They seemed sympathetic and asked a lot of questions. Including, of course, "Where is his father?" I believed they were interested and concerned for Steven. I didn't realise I was only giving them ammunition.

I'd been told that Steven would settle in and get used to the routine soon enough. He never did. He cried every morning for months. So did I. At home. At the school. At first the Evil Twins seemed kind and patient. They said they understood how hard it was for me to see him sad. But, they said, I wasn't to worry. They could handle him and he was fine, really.

"He stops crying as soon as you leave," Tweedle-Dumb kept telling me. Bullshit. She was just saying it to shut me up. After a while, her patience began to wear thin and she started using words like Manipulation, Firm Hand, Spoilt.

The brainwashing commenced. They managed to convince me that Steven was the problem – that he was playing me, just being naughty. And, dammit, I believed them. They were the teachers, after all. I was just, well, a little girl. It's ridiculous the way I always buckle to any sort of authority figure. All it took was a sharp word in a firm voice, and I'd be doubting myself, bending over backwards to be the good girl. I put my child through trauma, because somebody with an opinion and a loud voice told me I should. I wish I could say I'm different now, but nah… I'd be lying. Great, big, giant chicken – that's what I am. Cluck, cluck.

Steven never misbehaved at school. He tried hard to do as he was told, to fit in. He was a quiet boy, quick to learn, but shy and reluctant to participate in group activities. They tried to force him, and he hated it. The more he cried, the harsher they became. They simply didn't like him.

Mom had warned me. She hated the place and we fought about it often. She thought I was being cruel, and I told her she was being too soft. I'm sorry, Ma. You were right. I should have listened. All my instincts told me I was crazy. But no, I was determined to see it through. If I gave up now and took him out of the school, what kind of spineless mother was I?

My heart said, "I know my son. He's a good boy. He would only behave this way if he was really unhappy."

My head said, "What do you know? You're a lousy teenage mother. Shut up and listen."

All the other children seemed fine. Only my child had a problem. It was a horrible thought – had I been bringing him up wrong all along? Had I really been spoiling him, as the teachers had been telling me? Maybe this was my fault, and what he needed was a stronger, stricter mother. How had I managed to get it all so wrong, when I'd been trying so hard to get it right?

The crazy Tweedles really messed with my head. They complained if he cried, if I picked him up, if I hugged him for too long or carried his suitcase. They bitched when he started writing his name, telling me I was pushing him and that he was doing it wrong anyway. They didn't want to hear about how he shone, about his interests or achievements. They didn't know him, and they didn't care. He didn't conform, and so he was wrong.

The pair of them took insincerity to a whole new level. In public, they preached God's love and how good it was to be saved. With a straight face. In private, they passed malicious comments about the children in their care, talked down to them, completely failed to understand them.

They were racist snobs. Tweedle-Dumber, about one of the families: "They're not actually that bad... for coloureds." Lovely. They started many sentences with, "I'm not a racist, but..."

When you hear those words, look out for white sheets and the lynching tree – they're never far behind. They thought they were the world's greatest mothers, while their own children were some of the most unlikeable kids I've ever met.

Two-faced doesn't even begin to describe them. And it was their tone of voice that confused me. I believed it all, because they sounded so sweet and sincere. They could make the most humiliating insult seem like heartfelt advice from a caring friend. God, I fell for it all. I'm so sorry about that now. I put Steven through nearly two years of hell, because I was too naive to realise that some people are just ***mean.***

When I heard they were studying Early Childhood Education (yeah, turns out neither of them was actually qualified as a teacher, at all), I decided I'd love to do it too. I enjoyed seeing Steven learn, it was exciting to watch him soak it all up. And I really loved spending time with him and other children his age. Teaching seemed like a good fit for me. I joined them on their course, and I did well. Really well, in fact. I aced my exams and my projects were great. The Ugly Stepsisters didn't like that one bit.

After receiving one of our projects back, Tweedle-Dumb said, "How could you get ninety percent? Ours are so much better. I mean, just look at it. I'd never give you ninety percent for that work. The lecturer doesn't know what she's doing."

Their blatant rudeness hurt me, but I tried to ignore it. They sulked and sniped, and I stopped telling them how I was doing. I couldn't believe that grown women could be so petty and jealous. ***Of me.*** It's really funny.

I don't know what possessed them, but once we'd finished studying, they offered me a teaching job. They'd managed to get rid of Miss Timid somehow, and took great delight in telling everybody what a terrible job she had done. I should have run a mile. I must have been stupid to think they wouldn't do the same to me. But I believed I was in no position to turn down a job, and nearly a year of listening to them had fucked up my judgment solidly, anyway. So I said yes, and I was excited.

I thought it would be perfect. Doing what I loved, getting paid for it (very poorly), and being with Steven all day. It didn't get any better than that. I was nervous, but motivated. I went in there with my beautiful theme posters and my weekly lesson plans straight out of the textbook, determined to be a better teacher than they were.

My first day was a disaster. It started off well enough, but descended into blood-spattered pandemonium. The morning went smoothly. Aunty Tracy (yep, the others had to make space for the new persona in my head) turned up and took control. She had a firm, teacherly voice, and she gave lots of hugs. The children liked me, I thought.

I was in charge of the little ones, some of them still in nappies. It was hard work – physically strenuous and emotionally draining. Besides flash cards and pencil grip correction, I did a fair bit of mopping up. Drool, poo, tears and red Mix-a-drink went everywhere. The job entailed crowd control, mostly, but we had fun. We sang songs, we did art, I taught shapes and colours, managing to get through the morning without killing anybody or inadvertently scarring them for life. I was encouraged – I could do this. I felt so good. Exhausted and sticky, but proud.

After lunch, everything turned to porridge. I was told to take the younger aftercare kids to the park up the road. There were about twelve of them. They lined up at the gate in pairs, and after ten minutes of lecturing them on road safety, we set off. In hindsight, I think it was a terrible idea to place the responsibility of a dozen two- to four-year-olds on the shoulders of a rookie on her first day – and off the premises, too. Actually, it's a terrible idea to have anybody do that alone. But Tweedle-Dumber told me they did it every day and it would be a doddle, so off we went.

All was okay at first. We played a few games designed to tire them out, and then I let them go off to play on the swings and jungle gym. I needed eyes at the back of my head. They were everywhere, and they were ***loud***. Terrified to lose somebody, I counted them constantly. I was refereeing an altercation between two small girls, when I heard a blood-curdling yell from the jungle gym. Little Christopher was lying on the ground screaming his head off. My knees went weak as I ran up to him and saw the blood pouring from his head. He had slipped off the jungle gym and had cut his forehead on a metal bar. To this day I can't stand looking at those monstrous death traps – I get heart palpitations whenever I see children playing on them.

Somehow, I managed to round up the scattered kids, grabbed Christopher and ran back to the school. I tried to hide the blood and my panic from the other children, but inside I was freaking out. Fuck, fuck, I'm going to get fired on my first day! Oh my God, what if he's brain-damaged. What am I going to tell his mother? Help, help, help! I've killed a child! Who the hell left me in charge? Are they crazy?

The thirty-second journey back to the school seemed to take forever. At last we arrived, thank God, without losing anybody along the way. I burst into the classroom and thrust Christopher into Tweedle Dumb's arms before breaking down. Through heaving sobs and hysterical apologies, I tried to explain. It took hours and litres of sugar water to calm down. I think I was more traumatised than poor little Christopher, whose mother arrived to take him to hospital. All stitched up, he was back at school the next day, proud of his battle scars. So, my first day as a teacher was also my worst experience as a teacher. I literally scarred a little boy.

I still had a job, though I would have given anything to never go back there again. But I did, and it did get better. I loved my kiddies and enjoyed seeing them grow and learn, knowing I was helping them.

I resisted all the Tweedles' attempts to convert me to happy-clappydom, but I took perverse pleasure in their irritation at my blank stares as they tried to convince me that I needed Jesus in my life. I would smile and nod, listen intently, then go on my merry, heathen way. I loved to piss them off by leaving Hare Krishna literature out on my desk for them to see. Aneurysms all round. Hilarious. They made my life hell, so I had to take my entertainment where I could find it.

After eighteen months, I had to leave – or run the risk of losing my mind, not to mention my natural aversion to inflicting grievous bodily harm. Steven was miserable, I was miserable, the money sucked. They were offended at my reasons for leaving – namely disapproval of their draconian teaching methods and their shite personalities, but I gritted my teeth and got through my notice period with my sanity just barely intact.

Steven thrived at his new school. It was astonishing to see the difference in his behaviour. Although he always remained shy and sensitive, the relaxed, caring environment did wonders for his confidence.

But while Steven was okay, I was, of course, jobless. Interview after interview for preschool teaching jobs followed, but all were far from home, with rotten pay. Taking any of those would have meant that I'd pay out of my own pocket for the privilege of wiping up snot ten hours a day. Not worth it.

Sad, but one must move on. And I was moving on in more ways than one. After three years together, James and I broke up. I suppose we'd drifted apart, as they say. We'd both grown up and changed, and although we cared about each other, it was the idea of each other that we'd been in love with.

Ours was a protracted, ugly, on-again, off-again break-up that went on for months. He loved my long hair. I cut it short. He hated my hairdresser. I dated him.

Getting over James took time – for years afterwards, my stomach still did that sick little ex-boyfriend-looking-happy-without-me lurch whenever I saw him. At the time, the idea of not being with him was foreign and painful. It also meant I had to abandon, for now, our shared dream of a white picket fence and a happy little family. Worst of all, Steven was losing the only dad he'd ever known.

But the question I had to ask myself was this: Was it James I wanted, or was it what he represented for me? Horrible as it is, I think I know the answer.

Chapter Nine

In which she drives the process, while remembering The Boys She's Done Before

Being an unemployed single mother is no fun, let me tell you. Neither is being a single mother employed by nutters. I had to do something about getting a new job that paid actual money. Preferably with a boss in possession of all his marbles. Wishful thinking? Well, yes. Since my teaching days, my bosses have seemed progressively marble deficient.

Teaching clearly wasn't going to work. My teacher's salary was so miniscule as to be embarrassing, on top of which I had to buy all my own teaching materials. When I left, I had a year's supply of empty cardboard egg cartons and no use for them. There are only so many piggy-masks a child wants to make before getting bored.

It was time to get real. I decided to do a short computer and secretarial course, and to embark on a stellar career in paper shuffling. For some weird reason, people are far more willing to pay proper money to women who type arb memos all day than to the ladies who look after their children.

I looked forward to a change and thought an office job might be cool. I almost imagined for a second that I could be a dynamic, driven career woman like you see on TV, balancing work and motherhood with consummate ease and sexy hair. Theme tunes from eighties movies played constantly in my head… ***Working 9 to 5*** and so on. Good grief. I was so ***dof***.

So I learnt how to drive a computer, how to type with more than two fingers (The quick brown dog jumped over the lazy fox – or was it the other way around?), how to make tea for the boss, how to do petty cash. When I thought of the real difference I'd made teaching, the meaninglessness of this new life grated me. But I was good at it without having to try too hard. I was organised and methodical (OCD can come in handy). The sane, sensible columns of numbers calmed me, soothed my frazzled nerves, as did purchase orders in triplicate and colour-coded filing systems. Sensible Tracy was as happy as a pig in shit.

Less than I'd aspired to for my life, but at least I knew I could handle an office job without making anybody bleed, except in gratifying daydreams where I'd shove the boss's head through a plate glass window. This and other lovely fantasies have kept me sane; there's nothing like contemplating bloody murder to bring a smile to your face on days when it seems everybody around you has eaten a bowl of stupid for breakfast. It works.

I passed my course well and a month after graduation I started my first job as a receptionist at a labour broking office. Reception work probably wasn't the best fit for me – a basic requirement is a bubbly, People Person type personality, something that is lacking in my make-up. Other qualities required for this particular position (which I also lacked) were the ability to swear loudly at people in four languages, martial arts training and Zen-like patience. A fuck you attitude in general would have been helpful. I didn't know this at the time. I was under the mistaken impression that working hard and being helpful would be enough. Even though the idea of talking to people (even friendly, happy ones) for eight hours a day – and smiling while doing so – made my stomach hurt. Still, beggars can't be choosers and I was grateful for the chance to start somewhere.

My illusions were soon shattered. My job was a far cry from what I'd imagined. It was about as glamorous as answering the phone at an Epping panel-beater – just a tiny step up from a stuffy prefab, decorated with tattered ***Scope*** pin-ups circa 1987. I'd pictured a new wardrobe filled with pastel shift dresses and coordinating accessories. I'd looked forward to lively boardroom meetings and sociable office camaraderie. Recognition for a job well done. Awe at my astonishing filing prowess. Record-breaking rise through the ranks to be promoted within months to head of Staple Procurement or something. Stuff like that.

What I got was an uncomfortable desk in a freezing cold hallway (on a raised platform, so that anybody standing in front of the desk could see right up my skirt, or up my jacksie, as one male colleague so eloquently put it), office politics so cut-throat it was a wonder anybody was left alive, a clunky old switchboard that nobody explained to me, and staff members who refused to take calls for weeks on end. I was the last frontier (or first line of defence, depending on how you chose to look at it) between enraged contract workers who hadn't been paid in six weeks and grumpy wage clerks who refused to come out of their holes to help resolve problems of their making.

In short, I'd been banished to hell.

Picture this: It's 3pm on a scorching Friday afternoon in January. Receptionist Tracy is congratulating herself on the completion of her first week as a working mother, and doing what all working mothers do all day long – watching the clock for home time and pondering just how badly this full-time job is going to screw up her child. I was beginning to think about packing up, when the front door burst open and what seemed like the entire Cape Town City Council's Cleansing Department streamed in, brandishing scruffy payslips and angry expressions.

Oh boy. Nervous as hell, I tried hard to be professional and to help them one at a time, but they were not interested in queuing. They wanted their pay issues – sorry, their ***Fokken Pay Issues*** – fixed immediately. They did not care who handed over the cash, but somebody was going to do it, and before they left the building, too. Twenty to thirty mean, sweaty labourers crowded around my desk, some shouting, others loitering and a lucky few leering up the jacksie. I was terrifically polite and tried to remain calm, but the tears were not far off. They wouldn't listen. What did they care if the wage office was closed for the afternoon? Which, of course, it wasn't. Those buggers were in there, all right, drinking coffee and laughing at the new patsy trying to make herself heard without being shot.

I tried, "I'm so sorry sir. I can't help you. The wage office has already closed and they're the only ones who can help you. I don't deal with the wages at all. You can either come back on

Monday, or I could take down your details and they can get back to you."

Well, that worked a charm. Fists came banging down on my desk and were shaken in my face. Threats were issued. Some of the more aggrieved gentlemen would not rest until they'd hunted me down and killed me. Fingers were drawn menacingly across throats, just in case the message remained unclear. Over and over I explained, politely and calmly, that I could not help them; I had no money to give them.

The mob just got more and more pissed off. So did I. Clearly, no help was going to come from anywhere on those premises. Everyone else in the office was suddenly busy, or had temporarily been abducted by aliens, it seemed. There was only li'l' ol' me. They should have issued me with a Kevlar vest along with my company stapler. Then again, riot-management wasn't in the job description.

After an hour of talking to the wall (if walls could curse and loom in an ominous manner), I was getting ready to fake an epileptic fit to get myself out of there. While the ringleader continued to berate me, my eyes began to roll back in my head in just the right way, while I worked up a good, frothy mouthful of spit. As I was about to drop to the floor, Elusive Boss Man sauntered in, all rugged good looks and starchy chinos.

Damn, was I glad to see him! My saviour! He'd get me out of this. And he did. He took charge of the scary guys and promised to sort out their money immediately. I was a little peeved that after all my attempts at professionalism and helpfulness in the face of insanity, all it took to pacify the mob was a drop of testosterone and a few off-colour jokes. Bloody hell. Still, they'd stopped threatening to stab me to death, so I guess we were all winners.

At the first whiff of Boss Man's Hugo Boss (coincidence? I think not*)*, the hitherto invisible wage clerks reappeared mysteriously, like ***The 4400.*** They bustled around efficiently, as if they hadn't been slouched over their empty desks for three hours, playing My Husband Is A Bigger Retard Than Yours. Have you noticed how many women do this? Bitching, moaning, whining, complaining, screeching hags. Awful. I'd love to ask them why the fuck they don't just leave if their husbands are such losers, but they'd probably eat me alive and accuse me of just being jealous because I Can't Find A Husband.

I got used to days like that. There were many. I also got used to the intestine-gobbling guilt that gripped me every morning as I left Steven. Even the mind-numbing exhaustion became second nature after a few weeks. I developed a slightly thicker skin and taught myself how to operate that crap switchboard. After three months, I barely flinched at threats against my person. I was efficient and took pride in my work, however pointless it seemed. I organised, filed and colour-coded the place into submission. I tossed old socks and leftover mince in Tupperware containers that I found hidden behind my computer, apparently abandoned by the previous receptionist. I put systems in place that nobody had thought of before, and sorted out admin messes that had stewed for months.

I Put Systems In Place… Yes, however much I hate that ludicrous, pretentious corporate jargon, I picked up some of it. It rubs off, you know, and one day you find yourself spouting absurdities like “owning the problem”, “driving the process”, “getting in on the ground floor” and other such cramp-inducing lingo. Without realising it, you turn into a “team player”, and actually believe that an afternoon of action cricket with a bunch of drunken colleagues is just the ticket to increase productivity. But be warned – once you reach that stage, only retrenchment can save you. Or sudden, violent death.

Some people thrive on that shit. I just think it’s stupid. I did my job to the best of my ability, but I never stooped to the “show-me-the-money” mentality. (Yeah, indeed, that phrase graced one of the so-called morale-boosting posters the company insisted on sticking up all over the place. Cheesy and so plagiarised. Shameful, really)

I guess I was never truly committed to, nor much interested in my job. This was no career – it was just a job and I couldn’t turn it into anything else.

After a few months, the company started a process of major restructuring. Sweeping changes were made. Retrenchment became a contagious disease. New logos were introduced, sales staff were renamed Business Development Officers – all laughable exercises in futility. Lots of knives lodged in lots of people's backs, and Boss Man left for greener pastures.

And so – meet the New Boss, infinitely worse than the Old Boss. New Boss Man was a domineering git with the people skills of a Spanish Inquisitor and the managerial ability of a wet mop. He was a large, sweaty man whose struggling arteries clanged audibly as he walked (it was cancer that got him in the end, although a massive Quarter Pounder-induced heart attack couldn't have been far behind).

Somehow New Boss Man combined blustery incompetence and despotic fussiness into one obnoxious package. He was also horribly paranoid, convinced that somebody was breaking into his office on weekends and going through his files. I don't know why anybody would want to do that, but he was sure of it, and he put forward a colourful assortment of conspiracy theories, using the word "mole" more than once. What these imaginary moles would be after is anyone's guess. He often spoke about getting the office phones "swept for bugs". Too many movies, perhaps, or maybe he did have people after him that we knew nothing about. The Doughnut Police, possibly?

He took to placing sticky tape over doorframes and hairs over filing cabinet drawers. Thing is, everybody in the office knew he did this, so we had great fun messing with his head. The guys in sales would unstick the tape and replace it slightly differently every time. Cruel, but deserved.

He wasn't a nice man, although looking back, I realise he was very much out of his depth. He was a numbers man: systems, procedures and paper trails turned him on. People scared him, and he was terrified of losing control of his staff, of not being respected. He was right to be terrified, so he compensated by being an utter bastard towards everybody. At least twice a week somebody would come storming out of his office, either swearing or crying. Husbands of upset staff members paid him angry visits too. Where other businessmen entertain important clients with expensive lunches and even more expensive lap dances (dodgy as it is, it seems to work), he once took the CEO of his biggest client to the movies to watch a weepy romantic comedy. Zero people skills, complete social ineptitude and absolutely no concept of personal space. Everybody hated him, poor guy.

For some reason, he seemed to have a soft spot for me. We worked closely together, God help me. On my birthday, he called me into his office and we had a private party with cake and fruit juice. He was a staunch Christian (another one!) and disapproved of alcohol. You can imagine what the rest of the office thought of this. I could picture their excitement as they peered through the keyhole looking for evidence of inappropriate behaviour. They loved that sort of thing. ***Eeeuw.*** Nearly lost my breakfast there. The image is too ghastly to contemplate. I never did it, okay? Let's just get that straight, right now.

New Boss Man would regularly lecture me on my choice in men and tell me I could do much better. He told me he could introduce me to any number of successful, respectable prospects. I never took him up on his offer, as even then I realised what a bad idea it would be to have your boss involved in your love life. It's possible that he just wanted to get some action himself, married and churchified though he was, but I'd like to think that his heart was in the right place. Oh, the awkward silences – what do you say to a boss who thinks he's mending your foolish ways with men? I was very young, and didn't know how to handle it. Now, at the grand old age of 28, I've discovered the Death Stare, which works remarkably well on nosy male bosses. Shuts them up faster than the mention of gynaecological procedures.

However creepy it all was, he was probably right about my relationship choices and gave me pause to consider All The Boys I'd Done Before. Not to mention the ones I hadn't and should have.

My first real schoolgirl romance was with a boy who loved his hair more than he loved me. I was twelve years old. It didn't last long, and that's all I can say about that.

The second boy was yummy – I couldn't believe my luck. He was a great, big, dumb lug of a boy, six feet tall at the age of twelve and a heavy metal freak. Not the sharpest knife in the drawer, but oh, the goose bumps! He taught me to appreciate Guns 'n' Roses and I tried to teach him how to spell. We first held hands at our school barn dance (do ***not*** say a word), and then spent the next three months in an unconscious liplock, emerging occasionally to write sweet letters to each other. I still have the letters he sent me. Shocking handwriting, littered with swear words followed by profuse apologies for the profanity. He also sent me heart-shaped "I Love You" stickers. The thought of him painstakingly sweating over a full-page letter to me made me feel unbelievably special. Before I entered his universe, the most he ever wrote was "Mr D Sux's", in spray paint on walls. He must have really loved me.

Of course, as these things do, the romance fizzled out once summer holidays were over. Rumours eventually reached me that an older girl, cool blonde Simone, was involved. Devastated, I was. Simone, you bitch. Our summer romance left me knowing all the words to Guns N' Roses' Patience, and with an abiding, morbid fear of Being The Last To Know. I still have both.

When he later tried to get back together with me, I wouldn't be swayed. By then I was into older boys who could spell. Dammit. Stupid, stupid. Multi-syllable words are all well and good, but they sure ain't gonna keep you warm at night. Should have stuck with him. His collection of tattoos is pretty impressive these days and he's also the Boy I'd Most Like To Kiss Again.

A string of mostly forgettable attachments followed. After the Boy Who Kissed Like A St Bernard came a brief fling with a neighbour – tall, blond, seventeen and delicious. He played the drums and was perfectly aware of how gorgeous he was. Innocent and virginal, I valiantly fended off his rigorous attempts to get into my pants. Of course, I was way too young to appreciate his tastiness. He was a bit of a bastard, really, but what a pair of hands on him! Ooh, missus. Sexy Neighbour Boy wins the title of Boy I Really Should Have Shagged When I Had The Chance.

The first Boy I Really Fell In Love With was fifteen, gangly, awkward, bitchy and sexy as hell. We called him Mr Bean, because he made us laugh. But who wants to sleep with Mr Bean? Me, apparently. Even though he was one of my best friends and therefore off limits, I went ahead and fell in love with him anyway. But He Just Wasn't That Into Me. Or he was gay, which was the general consensus. Who knows? Maybe I just scared the shit out of him.

Terrible idea to fall in love with a close friend. I must have been crazy, but I couldn't seem to help myself. I wanted him badly and I was determined.

I got my chance one night, sitting outside and smoking B&H with him (we thought we were cool, okay!). He lay on the grass with his head in my lap. I found myself holding his hand up to my mouth and kissing his fingers, one by one. I remember him saying it was nice… finally, this was it. This I could do. I couldn't talk to him without choking, I'd never tell him how I felt, but put him on his back under the stars and I was pretty damn close to heaven.

I don't know who kissed first, him or me. Minor detail. What mattered was that it was sexy and wonderful and if ever there was such a thing as a perfect moment, this was it. I felt with electric certainty that nothing – ***nothing*** – would ever live up to this. And all we did was kiss. Bloody talented, that boy.

Other suitors included, in random order, Very Dumb Lifeguard Boy, Arrogant American Boy, Boy Who Was Actually Still Married The Bastard, Guitar-Playing Political Hippie Boy, Delusional Boy Who Told Me His Parents Were Spies Or Something and Scary Policeman Boy. Not included are the random 2am-after-six-Hunters gentlemen – for two reasons. Firstly, because a girl's gotta know when to stop embarrassing herself, and secondly, importantly, because I can't remember their names.

Then there's my latest crush, and this is truly embarrassing. It's Robbie Williams.

Don't laugh! Sigh… I, too, was like you, not so long ago. I scorned his music and scoffed at the culture-starved ignoramuses who loved him. I thought I was better than that.

It happened one hot night in November. Channel surfing while waiting for the Veet Bikini cream to work, I stumbled upon a Robbie documentary. And was mesmerised. Yes, mesmerised. I lay there for an hour, Veet forgotten (by the way, when they say "Do Not Exceed 10 Minutes," they really mean it), drooling with lust. When the programme ended, I emerged from my trance bereft. I needed more, ***more,*** I tell you. It's the tattoos, probably. And those lines around his mouth – oh my, his mouth. Ouch.

Sigh… Now ***there's*** a Man I Would Pay To Have Meaningless And Degrading Sex With. I've collected quite a bit of his music lately, and I'm trying to like it, I really am, but my finger still itches to hit the "Next" button. Sorry, Robbie. To be honest, I just want to see you with your pants off, really.

As I said, New Boss Man's concern about my love life was not entirely unfounded. At that stage, I was going through a regrettable phase of swapping one guy for the next, like chain-smoking, except with men, not cigarettes.

Lesson One: office romances are no good. After trying it three times, I have finally got the message. It took a while, but I now know that Shagging Colleagues Is Frowned Upon. And with good reason. Makes everybody think you're a slag, for one thing. Even if you're not.

Number One was a guy thirty years older than me (yes, you heard right). We had a good time together, and didn't care if people looked at us funny. It ended after five months, and I don't regret a minute of it. We both understood that there was no future in it. We were just having a good time. There's a lot to be said for dating an older man, although I won't say it, because my mother is going to read this. He was an interesting guy with a fabulous Scottish accent. (I've always had a fetish for foreign accents, ever since my sexy French boyfriend when I was thirteen. Ah! Those green eyes, the perfect skin and the way he would read ***The Magic Roundabout*** to me in French… Yum).

My first date with Number One started with Mexican food and many jugs of sangria. It ended sometime the next morning with the nagging feeling that I'd shagged Billy Connolly. Everybody at work knew about our fling and took great delight in teasing me about it, no doubt gossiping viciously behind my back, too. I didn't care. We managed to keep it from New Boss Man for a while, as he would have had kittens. But he found out eventually.

He saw us leaving work together one afternoon. I saw him watching us for ages, and I knew what was coming. Later on, he stopped Number One on the stairs on his way back up to his office.

"So, are you and Tracy relatives or something? I often see you coming to work together," he asked.

I nearly choked on my own spit. ***Relatives?*** Was he joking, or was he seriously that naive? Or was he malicious enough to want to make us spell it out for him? The entire office went silent – everybody wanted to see us get fired.

Number One took charge of the situation smartly, as he always did. He wasn't intimidated by the horrible little man at all. They hated each other and I was often stuck in the middle. They fought about everything, just for the chance to be right. Jeez, if I never see another itemised cellphone bill in my life it will be too soon. Another reason why ***Cosmo*** writes all those articles about never dating colleagues.

"Actually, no, sir. Tracy is my girlfriend. We've been going out for a while now." All very matter of fact and calm.

Seeing New Boss Man's cheeks puff up and turn red, then purple, then a deathly shade of white was delicious. He was livid. I could see his mind working furiously, trying to find something in company policy forbidding such conduct. Unfortunately for him, there was nothing in writing. Unofficial company policy was Shag Everybody You Possibly Can, but actual relationships between staff members were unusual, so talking about the relationship between Number One and me was a delectable teatime treat. You can imagine the atmosphere in an office with an equal split between single women in their early twenties and married men in their thirties and forties. ***Gaaah.*** The stuff those people got up to. Much worse than me, I promise.

I was sad when we broke up, but it had to happen. Life at work was awkward for a while afterwards, but we got over it and ended up working well together again. We've lost touch now, but it would be cool to be his friend.

I'm very ashamed to say that Number Two followed close on his heels. Short-lived and ill-advised, this was an entirely different story. I chucked him just as soon as I discovered he was not actually separated from his wife as he'd told me. Don't like to think about that one.

Number Three – well. Here things get complicated again. You see, he is the father of my daughter. I don't have anything really horrible to say about him, really. The worst one can say is that he was in over his head. Still, getting involved with him was not my best decision ever. We were just wrong for each other.

I need to psych myself up to talk about this one. Gimme a second, okay?

Hang on: remind me again why I'm doing this? Laying my soul bare for the whole world to see? Revealing uncomfortable truths about myself, history I'd rather forget?

Since I'm not on drugs, I must be temporarily insane.

Chapter Ten

In which she gets knocked up again, if you can believe it

W sauntered (he sauntered, mostly, as opposed to actual walking) into reception one day and introduced himself as the new guy from the satellite office. Cute, I thought, but I was still dating Number One, Number Two sniffing around on the fringes, flirting his li'l' heart out. Everybody, including me, found W annoying at first. His swagger, ponytail and scratchy goatee got on my nerves. In fact, it was only after he cut this horrid thing off that I began to look at him a little differently. Facial hair has never done it for me, so I really don't know what I was thinking.

Being too occupied with Number One, then Number Two, I didn't give W much thought, especially ***like that.*** Besides, he had a girlfriend called Nicky. Now, here's something that has always bothered me. Why is it that every guy you will ever date has an ex-girlfriend called Nicky? Why, why, why? Is there a Nicky-The-Ex factory somewhere, churning out carbon copies of the same girl, to be distributed generously among the male population of a certain age? What's up with Nicky? I mean ***bleergh.*** The name gives me chills, and not in a good way. Other common Ex-GF names include Natalie, Kerry (fucking Kerrys, they're everywhere) and, oh yes, Kim.

And what kind of name is Tracy? Sounds like a single mother's name to me. Do I know any married Tracys? I don't think I do. Makes you think, doesn't it? Bygones.

W and I ignored each other for a few months, then one day something clicked. Number Two had since left the building – he'd resigned and we were trying half-heartedly to keep in touch. Half-heartedly indeed, as I believe it was around this time that he crawled back to his wife. Grrr. I swear on my life I didn't know they were not properly separated.

It was one of those long, hot summer days at the office. The boss was away and the sexual tension was so thick in the air, you could have cut it into chunks and used it to stuff mattresses. Everybody was bonking everybody else, or trying to, apparently. The whole place was one fiddle away from a bankrupting sexual harassment lawsuit. The whole office sat around talking about W's girlfriend situation: he said he was unhappy and didn't know what to do. The resident agony aunt gave him some good advice, and he was on the phone to poor Nicky that very afternoon. We need to talk. Yikes. Such a ghastly phrase, yet so versatile.

Flirting began in earnest. There were innocent back rubs (ha!), much playing with hair (his now cut short and spunky) and sitting on laps. Shudder to think of it now. The innocent back rubs culminated in a not-so-innocent kiss behind closed doors in the debtors' clerk's office. She was out smoking weed on the roof, I think.

We started dating properly shortly after. Dating a guy who was basically still a kid was a culture shock after being with Number One, who was older than both my parents. In fact, W was a little younger than me, something I'd never tried before. Now I know why. I was a mother with responsibilities, he was a party boy, just barely twenty-one. We had almost nothing in common and struggled to find things to talk about. We solved that problem by not talking much at all. It was difficult to have a conversation with him that was not punctuated by sound effects anyway. Existential discussions about the universe and philosophy were not our forte. Our attention was elsewhere. Ahem. I'll never forget those dreadful movie posters stuck all over his room – it's pretty difficult to get your groove on while ***The Crow*** is staring at the back of your head. Those eyes followed me everywhere, I'm telling you.

There are benefits to dating a younger guy, too – different, but no less impressive. Those benefits kept us together just long enough for me to delude myself into thinking we had something real. It worked for a while. The problem came when I began to daydream about something more. I wanted the same things I always had. A "proper" family and a home of my own. To no longer be a burden on my parents. I wanted a man who would love Steven as his own. Someone with whom I could be connected and truly comfortable, somebody who would ***get it.*** Back in those days, I still believed such a man existed.

W told me he wanted those things too. He said he could give me what I needed – could, and wanted to. I believed him, despite all evidence to the contrary. I'm really good at talking myself into things I know are crazy, stubbornly determined to make it right, no matter what. What a terrible habit. I was barking up the wrong tree entirely – it couldn't have been more wrong.

He tried hard to get along with Steven, but it was a strain for both of them. That worried me, but I told myself they just needed time. He found it very difficult to relate to a young child – he couldn't get down to Steven's level at all, although you'd think it would have been easier for him from his youthful vantage point.

He just didn't understand. I'll never forget the day I bought Steven's school uniform for Grade One. I was so excited – any parent will tell you it's a big day. We arrived home and made Steven model his uniform and school bag up and down the lounge in front of the whole family. We were having a great time – until I looked over at W and saw how bored he was. He could barely conceal his irritation. He simply didn't get the big deal and had much better things to do. Like playing pool, or swanking about in his black trench coat or something. My heart sank when I saw his face, and yet I kept at it. God, I was so wrong to put myself and my child in that situation. I could kick myself for the wasted months, for the time and effort and tears I put into it trying to make it work, when it was plain from the beginning that it never would.

After a few months, we were spending every weekend at W's house, which felt like my own. Steven had his own bedroom there. I did grocery shopping every weekend, cooked and cleaned, and otherwise played house. Tension arose when I realised that W and his unemployed housemate were scoffing down all Steven's cereal and healthy veggies during the week. I'd spend half my salary on making sure that Steven ate well, and they just used it all. They never bought any food – before I came along, I think they lived on rice and cheap red wine. The house was a mess – I spent most Saturdays cleaning, with no effort being made to help me.

For months, I bristled with resentment, believing they should have been contributing as well, but now I realise I was stupid. They never asked me to cook and clean and look after them. I took it upon myself. I cleaned because I didn't want to live in filth, I shopped because I didn't want Steven to starve while he was there, and I cooked because I wanted to eat. And yes, I admit it – I loved it. I relished the role of Proper Mommy. I thought they would appreciate all I was doing. It turns out that they didn't give a shit whether I turned up or not. Maybe that's a bit harsh – they weren't bad guys, just typical twenty-two-year-old party animals who wouldn't know who Mr Min was if they found him eating their dinner. Who can blame them for that? I can't blame W for any of it, I suppose. I just chose poorly, wanting him to be something he wasn't.

He did everything I told him to do. I most definitely wore the pants in the relationship, so to speak. I felt safe that way. As long as he was under my control, I could make things work the way I needed them to. Yeah, I don't need Dr Phil to tell me that's a damn stupid idea. I walked around for months fantasising about the home and family we'd have. I budgeted and saved and planned our life together. The problem was, I was alone in doing so. W was just going along with whatever I said, telling me what I wanted to hear.

I was doing all the work – all the decisions were mine and so, too, the responsibility. If you come right down to it, my nagging was the only thing that kept our relationship together. He was just along for the ride.

But wait! There's more! And it makes me feel like such a bloody fool.

We decided to get married. Where was my mind? There was no proposal as such. No bended knee or romantic expressions of tender, undying love. (Damn it! When am I gonna get some of that! WAAAAAH!!)

No, what I got (lucky me) was, "Hey you wanna get married?" And right back to the Playstation. Do you know the worst of it? I said yes! Silly twit.

I truly have no-one to blame but myself.

My parents could not believe I'd actually want to marry the poor guy. They had a hard time adjusting to the fact that W and his long-winded boarding school stories were going to be around forever. So did I, come to think of it. Again, wrong person, wrong reasons, wrong everything. And I knew it was wrong. I knew it right from the start. But by now I'd got myself in so deep I couldn't bear the thought of admitting I'd screwed up again. So I pressed on.

Even in the midst of my half-hearted, feeble wedding planning, I wasn't happy. I honestly thought that this was the best I could do. I didn't know it wasn't supposed to be that way. I thought it was normal to feel claustrophobic and misunderstood and not heard. I believed that for a long time. How sad is that?

Nobody believed it would last. Not even my gigantic, family heirloom engagement ring could convince them otherwise. Everybody knew. They were probably taking bets.

And then – horrors! Those damn little pink lines on the home pregnancy test. Again. Goddamn. I don't know how I do it. My body seems to crave babies – my uterus cooks them up with glee. I was on the pill, so heaven knows how it happened. Remind me not to try ***that*** again, please.

So, now there was a baby on the way – even more reason to make it work, no matter what.

I don't know why I stayed. I have no clue why he stayed. Looking back, I know he didn't really want the things I wanted. What he was thinking is anyone's guess, actually. And to add insult to injury, I couldn't get him excited about the baby at all. Not like I was. I gave him tons of pregnancy and baby magazines to read, but I doubt he ever picked one up.

Whenever I looked at that untouched pile of ***Your Pregnancy*** magazines next to the bed, my heart ached. They seemed to symbolise every wrong decision I'd ever made.

"Now you're bringing another child into the world to suffer the consequences of your ridiculous choices!" they seemed to shout every time I passed. It hurt so badly.

For all his obliviousness, W agreed to be with me at the birth. The poor sap didn't know what he was getting himself into. I tried to prepare him for it, speaking about it all the time, but he never asked any questions (at least, no intelligent ones that didn't involve sound effects); he just listened until I shut up, and then didn't think about it again until the next time I brought it up.

I was desperately unhappy, and the cracks were quickly starting to show. He'd make some crude, infantile joke about giving birth, completely missing the point, and I'd just stare at him, thinking, "What the hell are you doing here?"

What did he really want? I still don't know. Maybe, like me, he was also a master of self-delusion and denial. We could have started a club, with badges and everything. We'd have members all over the world. Much like "Bobs International", a worldwide organisation of men called Bob. I swear it's true. I saw it on TV once, years ago, and have never forgotten it. Why not Petes International? Or Dicks Incorporated? Plenty of potential members for ***that*** club. I know a few.

We were both young and stupid. To think I could ***will*** something so fundamentally wrong into being right. Then again, it's not necessarily an age thing. I've seen many a forty-year-old divorcee squeezing herself into jeans two sizes too small on a Saturday night, desperately hoping it would help her nab Mr Right. Or Mr Good-Enough-For-Tonight, at least. Like them, my judgment on matters romantic has always sucked, big time.

W has changed a lot over the years, and I'm proud of the dad he has become. But back then I could have strangled him to death for being such a giant doofus. He meant well, but just couldn't give me the support I needed. I couldn't rely on him. I was on my own, basically. Again.

Everything fell apart a couple of months before Maria was born. After weeks of crying, ultimatums, discussions about money and the lack thereof, I'd finally had enough. We broke up. I gave back his enormous diamond ring, and got on with the business of bringing yet another child into my parents' home.

It killed me to do that. The idea of going crawling back to Mom and Dad (pregnant again, for fuck's sake!) made me absolutely sick. But I had no choice. That's probably why I stayed with him for as long as I did.

My guilt about doing that to my parents still weighs heavily on my mind. I don't know how to let go of it. Maybe I won't ever be free of it. God, Is there ***anything*** I don't feel guilty about? Some days it seems like everything is my fault – from my children's dubious father figures to global fucking warming. Probably not a healthy outlook. Somebody, tell me how to change that, please. Hopefully someone who doesn't charge by the hour?

***

Voluntary retrenchment is a beautiful thing. When I was seven months pregnant, I left my job with the New Boss Man and had six weeks at home before Maria was born. Oh, what a wonderful time! I loved being home with Steven, taking him to school and spending time with him in the afternoons. Just being around and present when he needed me was an amazing privilege. I'd dearly love to have that again.

It was immensely liberating to know that I didn't have to go back to that soul-destroying, sick office again. Colleagues still phoned me several times a week, though: "Where are the waybills? "How do I send a fax?" "What happened to that yellow Post-It note I left on my desk six months ago?" "Why is my head so far up my arse?"

Maybe they just missed me. I'd left them a detailed manual with instructions on everything from how to replace printer cartridges to how the CEO took his coffee. I doubt they even looked at it. Ha! I loved the fact that I never had to see any of them again.

I waddled around the house for six weeks, growing steadily more enormous. I was much bigger than I'd been with Steven. I just seemed to spread out everywhere. Possibly also had something to do with the fact that I had more money than I did when pregnant with Steven – money for crucial stuff like McDonald's and Nik Naks. Mmmm. Yum. It was the height of summer and I was damn hot. Towards the end I, couldn't do much except sleep and sweat and eat ice by the tray-load. Finally, just as I thought I would burst if my skin stretched any further, I went into pathetic, weak, laughable labour one Monday afternoon.

Concerned that this labour would progress unnoticed and as rapidly as the first and I'd end up giving birth in the car, I took myself off to the hospital way too early. I mean really early. Embarrassingly early.

The nurses laughed at me when I arrived, suitcase in hand, with almost no contractions. They told me to go home and come back later that night, when the labour was more advanced and I had something real to show them.

I refused. Not a damn was I going to leave that hospital without a baby. So I stayed, much to their annoyance. I was having contractions, but they were slight and manageable. Uneventful hours dragged on, and I began to realise that this time would be different.

Matters eventually did progress. I'd arrived at the hospital at 6pm, and by 11pm, I was finally in pain. Not a minute too soon. I was just about to admit that it must have been a false alarm. The pain of the contractions was much worse than it had been with Steven, and again I was having no pain relief. This time, however, I would gladly have gotten high on that happy gas if someone had offered it. Around 2am I called the nurse.

"Please, isn't there some gas or something I can have?" I must have sounded pretty desperate. She nearly laughed in my face.

"No, my girl. We've got nothing here. Come on, it's not so bad. Everybody else is doing fine."

Government hospitals. Hmph. Everybody else was doing fine because they had no choice. I don't think the labour ward had so much as a Disprin to offer.

Beds were in short supply, so I was labouring in the maternity ward itself, in full view of three other women who had just given birth. I walked up and down the passage for hours, bending double as each contraction gripped me.

I'm afraid to say, W was being no help at all. I'd prepared him for this. I'd told him how it worked, given him all the information he could have needed. But he still had no clue what was going on. He was completely panicked and seemed on the verge of tears all the time. When you're in the clutches of a side-splitting contraction, it's no time to be making other people feel better. He was pissing me off, big time.

His most glaring fuck-up was when he went home to get pillows for me. He came back with pillows, all right, but also with his housemate and his housemate's brother in tow. He'd brought them to say hi, he said. Say hi? ***Say hi?*** I'm supposed to entertain these people ***now***? Make small talk about the weather, while I wait for my waters to break and I'm in so much pain, I can barely breathe? What the fuck?!

I saw my visitors at the other end of the passage, looking sheepish and hesitant. They knew they had no business there. I reckon W brought them to keep him company. Jesus, I was angry.

He still didn't get the fact that this day was not about him. Entirely unable to think past his own discomfort, he was letting me down. ***Again***. I wanted to scream. I wanted to slap his silly face. I wanted to shake him and yell, "It's only one night, for fuck's sake! Just get over yourself and help me. Please!"

Murderous rage is definitely not conducive to relaxed labour. Messes with endorphin production something awful.

I got through the worst contractions by reciting Harry Potter spells under my breath. W thought I was crazy. I held his hand and squeezed it blue while he gibbered and shook. This wild, out-of-control mad woman scared the bejeebers out of him.

The spells worked a treat, actually. I reckon ol' JK should look into the doula business, should her current millions ever run out. My body was working well, all progressing according to plan, and now it was only a case of getting the child out of me. Sounds simple, hmm? I was proud of myself, actually. No pain relief, none of that lovely gas that takes the edge off and makes you higher than… well, really high. It was just me and my child and Mother Nature, doing it together.

At about 4am, W announced that he was too tired to go on. ***He*** was too tired? He who had been sitting on his ass for hours, holding my hand, while I squeezed an object the size of a medium watermelon with sharp pointy fingernails down my fucking birth canal? The lazy, useless ***TOSSER***! Yes, he was exhausted, he told me in all sincerity, like I should understand. It had been a long day. He was going to nap in the car. He said he'd call my mom to stay with me.

He left. Can you believe it? My heart would have broken again, had it not been for the other bits of me that were busy tearing.

The day your child is born is supposed to be a joyous occasion. Nobody should have to deal with disappointment and sadness like that.

I've never been so glad to see my mother in my life. I cried when I saw her. At last, here was someone I could rely on. She'd help me. She'd understand. And she did, of course.

"I need to push!" I yelled at anybody who would listen just minutes after she arrived. Nurse arrived to check me out.

"Nonsense," she declared. "It's not time yet. And stop making such a noise; you're disturbing the other mothers!"

Fuck you, bitch.

She went away. I yelled again.

"I need to push! Somebody! Please!" Nobody came. I sent my mother out to find somebody wearing a uniform who could catch this baby that was about to come bursting out of me like that ***Alien*** thing. I've said it before and I'll say it again: you ***know*** when you need to push.

A couple of nurses moseyed on in, spotted my red, straining face and sprang into action, gloves a-snapping. I pushed beautifully. I felt so aware, so awake and in control. I've never felt so alive in my life.

And then, five minutes after I'd started pushing, I met my daughter. Laughter bubbled out of me as I gave that last push and someone called "Hello baby!" There is no other such feeling in the world. I felt so honoured. I sat up and picked my baby off the bed, still attached to the placenta inside me, and I felt in the presence of something else again. I don't know what that something is, but I'm truly grateful for it.

She was a perfect little girl – strong, healthy and beautiful. She was Maria, which means dark in Arabic. Her skin was rosy and she had dark hair and long pianist's fingers. I get all teary eyed when I remember seeing her for the first time.

Steven had a sister. I was a mommy of two – very different to a mommy of one, which might be termed a fluke. Mommy of two is the real deal.

My mother left immediately to fetch W. I was sorry that he'd missed it, but happy that my mother had been there to witness the birth. She still marvels about it today – how she saw Maria's little hand come into the world first. Some things are so special they just cannot be adequately described.

I started breastfeeding straight away. Quite an experience having your nipples manhandled by strangers. The nurses (even the bitchy one who'd told me to shut up) helped a lot, and encouraged me to persevere. Breastfeeding is the most rewarding thing I've ever done as a mother.

Two hours later, I was up and about, showering and feeling human again – none of the fainting drama I'd had with Steven. I was as strong as an ox and knew what I was doing. The nurses left me alone to do my own thing with Maria.

This time, at twenty-three, I was the oldest mother on the ward – a maternity ward veteran. The other girls were about sixteen or seventeen. It felt strange watching them with their babies. There was so much I wanted to say to them. And yet, I knew they wouldn't want to hear it. They seemed uninterested in their babies, so detached from the miracle they'd just experienced. They spoke about partying and friends and drugs. They left their crying babies for ages, while they wandered around the ward, leaving me to look after Maria and three others. They weren't ready to be mothers, and their children were probably destined to live their mother's lives over again. Watching them, I understood what everybody feared for me. It was sad to see. I wonder where they are today. I wish I could it fix it for them.

***

We left the hospital the next day, all the unpleasantness, guilt and drama of bringing another baby into my parents' house dissipated. There was only Maria and Steven – and our time together. We were a family of three, now. Steven took to his sister immediately and, even at seven years old, was a huge help. He was, and is, an excellent big brother. I'm so proud of him.

The four months at home with Maria were sheer bliss. She was an easygoing baby who slept a lot. When she wasn't sleeping, she was attached to the boob. I loved every minute of being at home with my children, and dreaded the day I'd have to find another job. That day came, though, as inevitable as the taxman.

Now I had to leave my two darlings at home every day to travel by train for an hour to a crummy job with, honestly, the craziest woman you could ever hope to meet in your life. All my previous bosses paled by comparison. I'm terrified she'll read this and sue me, so I will say no more. Except that she should have installed a revolving door in her building, the staff turnover was so mind boggling. I lasted six months before I threw in the towel. Which were five-and–a-half months longer than anybody else before me.

Six months of expressing breast milk every lunch break (can I hear you say ***Moo***?), then racing home after work to catch Maria before she fell asleep to give her evening feed, spending two hours with Steven before he went to bed, squeezing in homework, supper, bath time, quality time, randomised nagging. Six months of stress, anxiety and exhaustion. I was trying hard to find that miraculous balance all those smug working mothers brag about. Balance? As far as I'm concerned, balance is for skinny, double-jointed women wearing spangled leggings. Do you see any bloody spangled leggings here? I think not.

Chapter Eleven

In which she reveals her secret identity: Ladies and gentlemen, boys and girls, I give you The Girl Who Couldn't Say No

It was a narrow escape from the World's Looniest Redhead. She was a cross between Bree Vanderkamp, Eva Braun and Dolly Parton coming off Prozac. Those prodigious jugs made my eyes water. I can't imagine what they did to her posture.

My two-week notice period dragged on and on. Many a time I was tempted to just get up and walk away, especially when she launched into the "You–Ungrateful-Bitch-After-All-I've-Done-For-You" speech, or any of a number of creative variations on the theme, "I Was About To Fire You, Anyway" and "You'll Never Amount To Anything" being just two of them.

I couldn't bring myself to storm out, though I'd planned my dramatic exit perfectly – a stirring monologue, with a few scathing close-to-the-bone insults thrown in for good measure. But as you know, I'm a gutless wimp. I didn't do any of those brave, satisfying things. Instead I gritted my teeth, swore a lot in my head and stopped eating. Great for losing post-pregnancy fat, terrible for mental health. Walking out of a job before the agreed time was something Sensible Tracy and her cronies just wouldn't allow. Only irresponsible people did that sort of thing and, God knows, I had enough black marks against my name already. In a sick, masochistic kind of way, I was proud of myself for sticking it out as long as I did. How wretched is that? I'm telling you, people, it was a madhouse. It was like ***A Clockwork Orange,*** and I'm not talking about her hair.

I moved on to a pleasant new job with a small company that did obscure Internetty sorts of things, impossible to explain to random wrong-number callers. This was my first "good job" that wasn't a dead-ender with no prospects.

And what a difference it made to my life. I put on six kilograms (thanks to Engen QuickShop… choccie brownies, mmm…) and was longer chronically dehydrated due to Crazy Lady's "No-Drinking-At-Your-Desk" rule. No paranoid delusionals, no religious freaks and zero shagging prospects to distract me from the task at hand. Peace and quiet; a real job, at last.

Just me in my office, nobody to bother me, spewing out Excel spreadsheets until my little heart burst. It was wonderful. For the first time ever I was happy at work. I was good at what I did and I was learning new skills. And, oh happy day, I could walk around barefoot in the office and nobody cared. As much as I like looking at fancy, professional-looking strappy heels, the fuckers are a bastard to wear. Gimme my Tigger socks, any day.

There were no rules for eating, drinking or toilet usage, no conspiracy theories and no bipolar cases. (That I knew of, anyway.) Unlimited Internet access (woo hoo!) and sympathy for my parental responsibilities made it a very cool place to work. Regular hours (I was out of the door and on the pavement by

16h27 every day) meant I was always home in time to do the required Mommy Things with the children.

Of course, I had plenty of help from my family, especially Mom. But I tried very hard (and still do) not to take advantage of that, with varying degrees of success. I'd had it pretty easy, all things considered, so making life harder for myself seemed the logical thing to do. I've been known to jump out of bed in the middle of the night and run around the house picking up toys in my sleep, just in case Mom woke up and noticed something out of place. I'd have two school lunches made and one uniform ironed before I woke up. It's a special talent, but doesn't make for restful nights. No wonder I look like shite half the time.

Mom looked after the children while I worked, so I managed to avoid sending them to aftercare. That suited me, since it was a saving and I knew my children were happy in their own home with their granny who loved them and who wouldn't force them to eat beetroot under pain of death, as had happened to poor Steven during his heart-warming days at the Preschool of Hell. That terrible place probably contributed massively to Mom's hatred of the idea of aftercare. I think she believes children in aftercare are used as cheap labour to make Levi's or soccer balls. And there you were blaming Malaysia. Tsk tsk.

Mom is a different sort of granny – not the knitting, baking, shawl-wearing type. She prefers ***Tomb Raider*** and sword fights and building her own steps. She doesn't cook if she can help it and I've never known her to embroider anything.

The two of us are very different, yet in some ways so similar it's frightening. Two grown women in one house is a daunting business, and I feel sorry for my dad sometimes. He usually tries not to take sides when we fight. Dad is the Switzerland of the Engelbrecht family, preferring to mediate, while calmly and rationally considering both sides of whatever battle is being waged. This sensible, mature approach usually earns him withering scorn from both sides. Then, in the face of our combined derision, he'd scuttle back to his couch, a beaten man, leaving us to our Mexican stand-off over the correct way to iron a shirt.

We make things complicated for ourselves, Mom and me. Still, I owe her a lot, and I will always be grateful for the peace of mind she has given me, and the years of her life she has given my children. Thanks Ma.

In the early days at my new job, stress that I'd been living with ever since my relationship with W just melted away. My hair, which had been falling out in clumps thanks to Crazy Lady, began to grow back. The regrowth was all patchy and weird, but an improvement on the bald spots, so who am I to complain?

It felt as if things were coming together for me, at last. I felt like a real grown-up. I thought I could go far. I thought that in two or three years I'd be able to afford my own house, a car – a proper life, in general.

Nearly five years later, I'm still sitting on the same chair (worn a bit under my left bum cheek), drinking the same coffee and stretching the same budget as I was back then. Gimme an R!!

Gimme a U!! Gimme a T!! Whaddaya get? Comfort zone is the term, I believe. Or maybe it's Lazy Arsehole. What do you think? Voting lines now open.

As far as W was concerned – we were officially Not Together And What A Lucky Escape. We'd both moved on nicely, and with some relief. The resentment and negativity of our last few months together had given way to a kind of guarded politeness. We weren't friends, but we'd resolved to be good co-parents to Maria. Or rather, I had resolved, and he'd tried to do as I told him. Things were rocky at first. We fought a lot in the first year, as he found his feet and learnt how to be a dad, and an adult, I suppose. Money, reliability, and priorities were the usual suspects. I still believed I could bully him into behaving. He had the parenting instincts of a chest of drawers at first, I'm sorry to say, and was still so self-absorbed that each time he opened his mouth, he risked disappearing up his own bum.

Maria scared W. He was tense and wooden, entirely unable to cope when she cried or didn't want to go to him. He must have dreaded his visits, sometimes. Not only did he have to be responsible for this terrifying, helpless child who couldn't explain what she needed, he also had to contend with the Bitch Ex-Girlfriend (um, that would be me) watching his every move and complaining bitterly when he stuffed up. Maybe all new dads (especially single ones) go through this. I was just terrified that he'd end up being another David.

Thankfully, things have improved over the years. Time, experience and love for his child kicked in and sorted him out good and proper. Thank God – otherwise I'd probably have thrown myself off a building – or him, on second thought. W has become the dad I always suspected he could be and Maria loves him. They bake Barbie cup cakes, his girlfriend calls her Pretty Girl and plays with her hair. They're doing fine. I'm proud of him for not being so furniture-like anymore. It can only get better, although I do wonder how he's going to manage her teenage years. Egad. She's going to cringe a lot, I bet. Poor child.

On the subject of fathers, I bet you want to know what happened to David. Honestly, for seven years or so, nothing. He was completely out of the picture, as though he didn't exist. That suited me just fine, in my more selfish moments. But I worried about the effect it had on Steven. He never spoke about David. Occasionally, I spoke to him about his dad, and asked him how he felt about it. Didn't he miss him? Didn't he wonder about him? Didn't he wish he had a dad like everybody else? Steven always said he was Fine. He was trying to spare my feelings, even at five, six and seven years old. I'm sorry. He's had way too much to deal with than seems fair.

Then one day, when he was about nine years old, during one of my random probing sessions, I asked if he'd like to make contact. He said yes. I was surprised, and nervous as hell. After making some enquiries through his ex-girlfriend, his mother phoned and gave me his e-mail address.

I didn't know how to react at all. I wasn't doing this for me – I was still angry with him, but couldn't allow my feelings to cloud my judgement about what was best for Steven.

When I wrote to him, my first question was, why. Why didn't he fight for his son all those years ago? Why didn't he come looking for him? Why didn't he try harder? Why did he find it so easy to just walk away?

I wasn't emotional. I wasn't rude. I just needed those questions answered before I could decide whether Steven would be safe pursuing a relationship with his father. He did answer me, in a way. He admitted he was wrong. He admitted to being immature and lazy and not knowing how to handle the situation. He wasn't defensive or angry, which deflated me a bit, actually. I expected a fight, but it never came.

We chatted via e-mail for weeks, me asking the hard questions. David didn't say too much. What ***can*** you say, really? Eventually, we tentatively decided that they would start corresponding via e-mail, just to see how things went. No pressure. I made David promise on his life that this is what he wanted to do. I questioned him long and hard about his motives and made it clear that he should not start something he had no intention of following through. I told him I would not let Steven be hurt again, and if he wanted to walk away again, this was his last chance to do so.

He hasn't. They've been in touch for nearly four years now. They e-mail, they speak on the phone. David sends presents for

Christmas and birthdays. Steven even spends time with David's mother occasionally.

Steven and David met face to face for the first time a few months after making contact. They hadn't seen each other since before Steven turned two. What an emotional day. They met at my office and I left them alone while to chat. Steven was shy and awkward, but underneath all that, I know he was happy to be with his dad, at last. That scares me, because I can see how much he wants to have his father in his life, and I don't know how it's going to turn out.

It's been a huge leap of faith – I have to have faith in David, which is hard enough, given the past. But I also have to have faith in Steven – faith that he knows what he wants and that he can handle it, whatever the outcome. That's a lot for a boy of not-quite-thirteen. My nerves are ***shot.***

So far, so good. It's not a regular father-son relationship, and it's doubtful it ever will be. But it's more than they'd had before, and that's good, at least. Whatever one can call it – friends or buddies or family – the two of them will have to define it for themselves, somehow. I'm sure Steven wishes for more and that breaks my heart.

He's brave, my boy. I love him so. He's turned out splendidly – even with a teenage mother who couldn't say no.

I think I'm supposed to say that I spent the next five years expertly juggling motherhood, career and personal fulfilment. I think I'm meant to be some sort of shiny example of dynamic, sexy, 21st century momminess. Are you waiting to hear that I have it all, and you can, too? Tee-hee. I could tell you that, of course, except I'd be lying through my teeth, and we all know it.

Show me a single mother with time to do her nails and drink Sauvignon Blanc in a candlelit bubble bath and I'll show you somebody who feeds her children McDonalds four nights a week. There's just not enough time in the day for that sort of luxury. That elusive Balance, you read about? It's an evil myth. There is no such thing. The best you can hope for is moments of sanity and equilibrium amid frantic juggling, a moment when all the chainsaws are up in the air and you think you know where they will land when they come down. Sometimes you're right, and sometimes you're… um**…** not.

As a single mother, something's gotta give. In my case, I've simply dispensed with the preposterous Me-Time charade. Me Time. Oh ***pulleez*** – pull the other one, it's got bells on. It's one of the biggest modern-day scams perpetrated against women the world over. Whose crazy idea was it, I'd like to know? Probably a committee of overtired, coked-up glossy mag journalist types, who dreamed it up one night in a desperate bid to fill 500 words between the Prada and Gucci ads, with a catchy headline designed to make us frazzled plebs buy more magazines. "Ditch The Guilt!" the windswept and airbrushed lovelies proclaim from the covers of glitzy mags.

Overjoyed to find something written that says it's okay to be tired and want a minute on the loo by yourself, you part with your R30 and flip straight to the headline page, only to find half a page of ridiculous, bullet-pointed ideas on how to Spend Time With Yourself. To pull them off, you'd need a staff of thirty and a parliamentarian's salary. Despondent and ashamed, you trudge home to your sticky un-Supernannied kids and two-minute noodles, while the magazine's smart-arsed words clang about in your head: Ditch The Guilt, Love Yourself, Eat More Lettuce… But you can't, even if that sequined nineteen-year-old on the cover said you should. Because, right or wrong, guilt is part of what being a mother is about. So now you feel guilty about feeling guilty. They're just making more rules for us, more impossible standards to live up to. Why can't everybody leave us mothers alone and let us get on with it in peace? I ask you. Screw you all, I say, and let us choose how we do it.

Me Time is a lovely idea if you have a nanny, a couple of housekeepers and pots of money. And a husband, preferably. If you have none of the above, an hour of Me Time a day simply becomes one more chore to add to your list. One more thing you have to fret over, when you fall into bed exhausted at midnight and scroll through the list of tasks you should have completed that day.

I've given up on the idea of special time set aside just for me, time when my children must bugger off and leave me in peace to read Jodi Picoult, or do Pilates, or whatever takes my fancy this month. I think it's sort of nasty, too. It's one thing to leave your children with the babysitter while you go to the movies. It's another altogether to make them feel like they're cramping your style at home. It simply doesn't work for me. A boozy bubble bath equates to one load of washing plus hanging time, or half a Barbie DVD with popcorn, or getting to bed half an hour earlier to drool unprettily onto my pillow. Honestly, which one are you going to choose? Who likes bubble bath ***that*** much, anyway?

What works is grabbing five minutes whenever I can to sit and stare into space, even if it means tuning out, for just one extra minute, plaintive cries from the bathroom of "Mommy! Come wipe my bum!" Cheese snackwiches for supper translates into an hour I don't have to spend in the kitchen – cucumber and apple on the side takes care of the balanced-diet issue.

My Me Time doesn't have a special name or a special timeslot. I take it when and where I can get it, and I don't feel like a failure when I don't get it. Now that's progress.

Epilogue

In which she gets a life and tries to live it

Well, there you have it. We're up to date. All that's left now is to tell you what's been happening lately.

As I write this, Steven has just started Grade Seven, close to the age at which my own story began. He's on the verge of becoming a teenager and that's hard to believe. I can't quite get my head around the idea that I could have a child of that age. Will someone please tell me what the hell happened?

I'm sitting here looking at the badges I need to sew onto his school shirts, wondering how I can possibly get out of doing it. I'm no seamstress. I can cook and bake and iron reasonably decently, but sewing is beyond me.

That little voice I heard all those years ago, the baby who told me I would be okay before he was even born, has grown into a smart, sensitive young man with size-nine feet – someone I look up to, figuratively and literally (he's already taller than me, and it's only going to get worse). I had a warm, fuzzy moment the other day when I heard one of his friends telling him he's got such a cool mom. I liked that. I've never been cool before, and I suspect I am now only because the other moms are Tupperware Tannies over forty-five –flipping ***ancient***, when you're twelve.

High school is just around the corner, and yeah, I'm terrified. He will probably go to my old school, which is going to be a bit of a mind-fuck for me, if you'll excuse my French. I've been back there a few times, for school variety concerts and so on.

It's smaller than I remember (much like my entire summer wardrobe from last year), but besides that it's like stepping into a time warp.

My old locker is still in the same place, I swear, still with the same graffiti on it ("Die, Yuppie Scum" and Joan Baez prose about goats). That same old tree is still standing in the quad – the one I used to hide my pregnant belly behind. Weird.

I've been into the girls' bathroom and stood in the very same spot where I told my friends I was pregnant. Standing there with my eyes closed, the smell of Jeyes fluid in the air, I could see the ghosts of those giggly girls. And I remembered the girl I used to be. I feel a little sad, for some reason I can't quite fathom. I don't miss that girl. She wasn't happy – she was terminally self-absorbed and kinda irritating. But I am grateful to her for everything I have become. I think she'd be proud. I think she knew it would be okay. I remember standing in that bathroom all those years ago and feeling like I wasn't alone. Like somebody out there was watching out for me. And somebody was. Just as I can sense the presence of that Teenage Tracy here today, I think she could feel me – the me I am today – that day in August, 1993. Far from finding it disturbing, I find these emotions pretty comforting.

I wonder if the teachers will remember me when I take Steven there to sign him up?

I don't want him to go through the shit I did but, realistically, it's likely he will. I hope, I pray, that when it comes time for me to help him deal with life, I will remember what it felt like for me. I don't know how much of a difference that will make to him, but I can try. That's all we can do. And hope our trying is enough.

It dawned on me this week that a lot of what Steven will be going through as a teenager is going to be new to me. I stopped being a teenager before I turned fifteen. I went straight from just-out-of-childhood to some kind of weird quasi-adulthood, almost overnight. I never did the stuff sixteen- and seventeen-year-olds do. I've never been there. It's going to be totally foreign to me, and I hope I don't stuff it up too badly for him. Will have to let you know how it goes.

Maria is five years old and in Grade R. She's already talking about Big School. I picture her in pigtails and a school dress way too long for her, and I want to cry. My last baby, almost going to school. Things change when your children go to primary school. From that very first day they're moving away from you towards their own lives; you realise one day you don't know everything about them anymore. You feel ***old.*** Don't laugh. I'm twenty-eight, but feel much older. Well, kinda. Mostly I just feel ageless (not timeless, which I think has something to do with Botox). People ask my age and I usually need a calculator to work it out.

Before you have children, you're the star of your life – ***The Me Show,*** with everyone else being the chorus. Then you wake up one day and the bastards have cancelled you and stuck you on the Series Channel. You've been reduced to recurring guest roles on other people's shows. And the weird thing is, that's okay. Really, it is. What you give up is nothing compared with what you gain. If you don't believe that, you just don't get it. Even if it sounds corny. Just can't be helped, it's true.

The rest of my family is doing well, too. Emma is now the proud mother of a happy four-month-old boy, Thomas. She has an excellent case of neurotic paranoia going on, good enough to rival my own. She's a fabulous mother – I look at her and see how I should have been doing it all along.

Being an aunty is really cool – all of the fun and none of the poo.

Mom and Dad seem to thrive on the grandchildren idea. We're still the strong, connected family we've always been. We're lucky. Not many families could have pulled ***that*** off and still remained close. Of course we fight – we always will. But we're a great team, and I know how much I need them all.

And me? What about me? For nearly thirteen years I was happy with my guest-starring role. Then, last year, something changed. Could have been some kind of quarter-life crisis, or maybe Mercury retrograded into the fifth house of Sagittarius or some ***kak***. Whatever. Major things have happened, not the least of them the Executive Decision that spaghetti-strap tops may still be worn, even if no weight were ever lost. One of the most freeing decisions you'll ever make, believe you me.

And I wrote a book, which, by the way, is pretty damn hard. I'm somewhat proud and it has definitely been good for me.

Nothing like re-reading reams of pages of me-me-me for the seventeenth time to swiftly extricate the head from the butt.

There have been some interesting developments on the, shall we say, ***romantic*** front. Yeah, let's call it that. Sounds so much better than blurting out, "I got laid! A lot! Yippee!"

I started dating for the first time in five years and, oh Lordy, save me from the gut-wrenching fear. Nevertheless, I kept at it and slowly my usual bolshie Ice Queen sensibility began to thaw. Very slowly. And not without a good dollop of white-knuckled resistance. But just long enough to get myself one of those boyfriend creatures. Not the crappy, budget version either – those that are cheaper and easier to find, but need replacing every three months. No. No more pennywise and pound foolish for me. I'm after the real deal. I think I've found it.

Oh my Gawd, I hear you gasp. How did she manage that? Does she still remember how it works? Truth is, nope. I did have some feminine wiles once, but they got rusty and fell off, so I had to rely on my sharp wit and sparkling personality to land myself a man. And a very lovely man he is too, even if I did find him on the Internet. The fact that my online dating profile included only a headshot probably helped. Full-length photos might not have got me out of the starting blocks.

And before you ask: Yes, there are many sinister stalkers in cyberspace. Gross, married men all looking for discreet daytime fun. And some lonely, desperate model-train enthusiasts dressed by their mothers. But that's a story for an entirely different book: ***How***

to get a single mother into bed… It would be a very short book. Hint: wash the dishes. What a good idea such a book would be – practically a public service. If there's anything we frazzled single mothers need to keep us sane, it's regular recreational sex with people who are not axe-murderers, child molesters or entirely ignorant of the female anatomy. And familiar with soap and deodorant. Preferably able to string two words together. Unless they smell ***really*** good. Then intelligent conversation is irrelevant.

But there are also plenty of ordinary, nice enough people that you might otherwise never get to meet. It's worth a shot, if you have half a brain and can distinguish between potential serial killer and potential husband. Um… I know. Quite similar and difficult to distinguish – just use your common sense.

It's still early days for Mr Cyberspace and me. (No, I ***was not*** looking at that wedding dress. Of course not! Are you crazy? Marriage? ***Pah***!). I'm not allowing myself to get over-excited, because I don't want to look like a gigantic, lovesick idiot in six months' time. There. Aren't you proud of my restrained nonchalance? Let me assure you, no more gushing from this baby.

Okay, okay. I'm lying and we all know it. I'm in love! I feel wonderfully gooey and happy. And yes, dammit, I ***was*** looking at the wedding dress. Put that up your jumper and smoke it.

We'll see how it turns out, I guess. Whatever happens, I know I'll be okay. That's a great thing to know. It means you can do anything, and not be afraid. I'm not such a cold, cynical bitch, after all. Not nearly as much as I used to be, at any rate. It's progress.

Would I do it all again? If I could go back, would I still choose this path? Would I choose to have a baby at fifteen, knowing what I know now? It's been a long, confusing, scary, exhausting road. I've doubted myself so many times. I've hated myself. I've felt alone. I've felt ashamed of myself at times. I've cried, convinced I couldn't do it. Who would choose that?

Me. That's who. I would do it all over again. I have a life now, though I sometimes don't know what to do with it. I'm still tired – I haven't had an uninterrupted night's sleep in thirteen years. I'm frequently Red Bulled up to my eyeballs, which isn't particularly healthy, but at least I'm not a ***tik*** head. I still try too hard to be perfect. I still have fantasies of being the world's greatest mother, writer, employee, daughter, fellatrix, all-round saintly-type person who can make Duck L'Orange out of her head. I want to be all of that, while maintaining my staggering wit and Botticellian loveliness. Stop sniggering, damn you. It still annoys me that I can't be all of those things, but I am learning that "good enough" means just that. Hardest lesson I've ever learnt.

The voices are still there: Sensible Tracy, Flaky Tracy, Sister Tracy... But I'm learning to override them now, just barely. It's a struggle every day, but I'm finally the one in charge – and although they don't like it, they're getting the message. I may doubt sometimes, but truly I know I've done okay, scary body mass index and sucky saintliness-index notwithstanding.

I can feel, with every tiny bit of my being, that this is where I am supposed to be. It's not tragic, it's not second best – it's perfect. My children and I, we were meant to be. I believe it, I know it. Nobody else has to agree, nobody else has to care. Nobody else has to feel it. Just us. And we do.

PS Oh, by the way. I can say no, actually. I say no all the time. I say no to drugs, to sex with strangers, to dodgy meat pies, to heavy lifting. That old Methuselah of a doctor who told me to go on the pill because I'm obviously one of those girls who can't say no had it ***so*** wrong. Rude man.

####

About the author

Tracy Engelbrecht is a writer and mother of two. She lives in Cape Town and doesn't grow freakishly large prizewinning vegetables, but she does do a nice lasagne and her children aren't in therapy yet, so things are going well. She hardly ever drinks pina coladas or gets caught in the rain, but she's working on it.

That's the official story. The truth is, of course, much less exciting.

I was once The Girl Who Couldn't Say No, but these days I'm mom and eternal tea-maker to a teenage son, and mommy and copious cuddler of a tween daughter – both unique specimens of delicious humanity, way cooler than you'd expect with me as a mom. Also, they're much older now than when this book was first written, so the adventure continues. I'm also blogger, a columnist and a Tweeter-in-training. What else? Ah, yes. Thinker, reader, pudding-fantasist, champion-napper and above all, a sensible girl.

Hopelessly inelegant and perfectly inappropriate for every occasion, I wear my awkwardness like a badge of honour. I have to. It's the only jewellery I own not made from macaroni.

I am also the founder of Young Mom Support, a support group for young and teenage moms in Cape Town, South Africa. All proceeds from every copy of The Girl Who Couldn't Say No go towards supporting our group and our moms. Thank you, you've already made a difference.

PS I've given up on the pina colada thing (see above). It was never me anyway; I'm much more a creme soda float girl. Wif sprinkles

http://tracyengelbrecht.com

http://youngmomsupport.co.za

Made in the USA
Lexington, KY
21 February 2014